Wiener Urtext Edition
UT 50237

CW01604224
Kingston upon ... es
WITHDRAWN
FROM STOCK
...OR SALE

Robert Schumann

Sonaten für Violine und Klavier
Sonatas for Violin and Piano
Sonates pour Violon et Piano

Band 1/Volume 1

Nach den Quellen herausgegeben von/Edited from the sources by/Edité d'après les sources par Ute Bär
Fingersätze und Hinweise zur Interpretation von/Fingering and Notes on Interpretation by/
Doigté et Notes sur l'Interprétation de
Christiane Edinger (Violine/violin/violon) und/and/et Peter Roggenkamp (Klavier/piano)

Wiener Urtext Edition, Schott/Universal Edition

Wiener Urtext Edition, Musikverlag Ges. m. b. H. & Co., K. G., Wien
Ein Gemeinschaftsunternehmen der Verlage Schott Music GmbH & Co. KG, Mainz, und Universal Edition, Wien

© 2003 by Wiener Urtext Edition, Musikverlag Ges. m. b. H. & Co., K. G., Wien · Printed in Germany
Vierte Auflage/Fourth Edition
ISMN 979-0-50057-257-2

INHALT / CONTENTS / CONTENU

VORWORT

Robert Schumann, dessen Schaffen dadurch gekennzeichnet war, dass er mehrere Werke eines Genres in direkter Abfolge komponierte, wandte sich im Herbst 1851, am Ende seines ersten Düsseldorfer Jahres, verstärkt der Kammermusik zu. Zwischen dem 12. September und dem 2. November komponierte er hintereinander, lediglich unterbrochen durch das Klaviertrio op. 110 g-Moll, seine ersten beiden Violinsonaten op. 105 a-Moll und op. 121 d-Moll.

Angeregt wurde er zur Komposition der ersten Violinsonate möglicherweise durch einen Brief des Gewandhaus-Konzertmeisters Ferdinand David, der am 18. Januar 1850 an ihn schrieb: *Deine Fantasiestücke für Piano u. Clarinette gefallen mir ungemein; warum machst Du nichts für Geige und Clavier? es fehlt so sehr an was Gescheidtem Neuen und ich wüßte Niemand der es besser könnte als Du. Wie schön wäre es wenn Du jetzt noch etwas derartiges machtest was ich Dir dann mit Deiner Frau vorspielen könnte.*[1]

Dieser Bitte kam Schumann nicht sofort nach, denn erst im September 1851 entstand die erste Violinsonate op. 105. Neben den Vermerken in seinem *Projectenbuch*[2] und auf dem Vorsatzblatt seines Handexemplars des Erstdruckes[3] gibt Schumanns *Haushaltbuch* detaillierte Auskunft zur Entstehung des Werkes:

12. September 1851	*Duo f. P[iano]f[orte] u. Violi.[ine]*
14. September 1851	*Für Viol.[ine] u. P[iano]f[orte].*
15. September 1851	*Zieml.[ich] fertig mit d. Sonate f. Violine*
16. September 1851	*Fleißig. – Fertig m.[it] d. Sonate.*[4]

Bereits wenige Tage nach der Entstehung lernte Clara Schumann das neue Werk kennen, aber erst nach der Rückkehr von Wilhelm Joseph von Wasielewski, der von 1850–1852 Konzertmeister des *Allgemeinen Musikvereins* in Düsseldorf war, fand am 16. Oktober die von Clara ersehnte erste private Aufführung des neuen Werkes statt, über die sie schrieb: *Es ließ mir keine Ruhe, ich mußte gleich heute Roberts neue Sonate probieren. Wir spielten sie und fühlten uns ganz besonders durch den ersten sehr elegischen, sowie den zweiten lieblichen Satz ergriffen, nur der dritte, etwas weniger anmutige, mehr störrische Satz wollte noch nicht so recht gehen.*[5] Und Wasielewski berichtete: *Im ganzen zeigte sich Schumann von der Ausführung befriedigt, nur das Finale konnte ich ihm nicht zu Danke spielen. Es wurde noch dreimal durchgenommen, doch Schumann meinte, er habe eine andere Wirkung von der Geigenpartie erwartet. Ich vermochte ihm nicht genügend den störrischen, unwirschen Ton des Stückes wiederzugeben.*[6]

So zeigen denn auch die überlieferten Quellen dieser Sonate, das Autograph und die Originalausgaben von Klavierpartitur und Solostimme von 1852, gerade in diesem Satz zahlreiche Unterschiede, die auf Korrekturen hindeuten, die in der heute verschollenen Stichvorlage vorgenommen worden sein müssen[7]. Die zahlreichen Änderungen machen deutlich, dass das Finale zunächst nicht ganz Schumanns Vorstellungen entsprach.

Nach einer Darbietung am 9. März beim Fürsten Reuß fand am 21. März im Leipziger Gewandhaus dann schließlich die erste öffentliche Aufführung statt. Weitere öffentliche Darbietungen zu Schumanns Lebzeiten sind nicht bekannt, was kaum verwundert, denn die Violinsonate gehörte im Verständnis des 19. Jahrhunderts in den Bereich anspruchsvoller privater Kammermusik. In diesem Rahmen wurde das Werk gespielt, worüber verschiedene Quellen Auskunft geben[8]. Nach Schumanns Tod sind sowohl aus den überlieferten Tagebuchaufzeichnungen Clara Schumanns als auch aus ihrer eigenen Programmsammlung[9] vor allem Interpretationen durch sie und Joseph Joachim bekannt[10].

Diametral entgegengesetzt zu den Einschätzungen aus Schumanns persönlichem Umfeld steht die negative Rezension des Wagnerianers Theodor Uhlig (1822–1853) in der *Neuen Zeitschrift für Musik* vom 17. September 1852, in der Schumann als *Manierist* und *Vielschreiber* bezeichnet und ihm fehlende Originalität vorgeworfen wird[11]. Dieses Urteil vermochte der Publizität und der Verbreitung des Werkes, das Anfang 1852 im Verlag Friedrich Hofmeister in Leipzig erschien, nicht zu schaden, was die Verkaufszahlen des Verlages belegen[12]. Ebenso sprechen die verschiedenen, nach 1860 herausgegebenen Bearbeitungen für eine Wertschätzung des Werkes.

Nur wenige Wochen nach der ersten komponierte Schumann zwischen dem 26. Oktober und dem 2. November seine zweite Violinsonate. Wiederum gibt das *Haushaltbuch* Schumanns detaillierte Auskunft zur Entstehung des Werkes:

28. Oktober 1851:	*Scherzo zur 2ten Sonate f. Viol.[ine]* [II. Satz]
29. Oktober 1851:	*Andante zur 2ten Sonate.* [III. Satz]
2. November 1851:	*Die 2te Son.[ate] ziemlich beendigt.*[13]

Allerdings schrieb Clara Schumann noch am 4. November 1851 in ihr Tagebuch: *Robert arbeitet fleißig an einer zweiten Sonate für Klavier und Violine. Ich brenne vor Ungeduld danach.*[14] So ist anzunehmen, dass das Werk im Arbeitsmanuskript bis zum 2. November zunächst nur skizziert wurde und erst in den folgenden Tagen vollständig ausgearbeitet worden ist. Die erste private Aufführung durch Clara Schumann und Wilhelm Joseph von Wasielewski fand am 15. November 1851 in Düsseldorf statt. Demzufolge muss in der Zeit zwischen dem 4. und 15. November die Sonate von Schumann endgültig fertiggestellt und kopiert worden sein, denn wegen der zahlreichen Streichungen, Korrekturen und Auslassungen ganzer Abschnitte im Arbeitsmanuskript wäre eine Aufführung aus dem Autograph nicht möglich gewesen. Bei der für diese private Darbietung benutzten Abschrift handelte es sich um die Stichvorlage und die beiliegende Reinschrift der Violinstimme. Die laut Wasielewski von Schumann im ersten Satz vorgenommenen Korrekturen, die in dieser Abschrift der Klavierpartitur enthalten sind[15], belegen dies.

Über das neue Werk notierte Clara Schumann am 15. November 1851 in ihr Tagebuch: [...] *sie ist wieder von einer wunderbaren Originalität und einer Tiefe und Großartigkeit, wie ich kaum eine andre kenne, – das ist wirklich eine ganz überwältigende Musik.*[16] Ebenso begeistert äußerte sie sich in Briefen an ihre Mutter Mariane Bargiel und den Freund der Familie Avé Lallemant.

Somit ließ Schumann etwa einen Monat nach Beendigung der ersten Violinsonate bereits das zweite Werk dieser Gattung folgen. Schumanns Bemerkung bezüglich der Ursache für die Entstehung des neuen Werkes [...] *die erste Violinsonate hat mir nicht gefallen; da habe ich denn noch eine zweite gemacht, die hoffentlich besser geraten ist*, ist wohl eher selbstironisch und weniger als Ausdruck echter Unzufriedenheit zu verstehen, denn sonst hätte Schumann die erste Sonate sicher nicht schon im Januar 1852 im Druck erscheinen lassen. Bereits der Titel des Werkes, *Zweite grosse Sonate für Violine und Pianoforte,* weist durch das Attribut *grosse* darauf hin, dass zwischen beiden Kompositionen Graduierungsunterschiede bestehen. Interessant ist in diesem Zusammenhang, dass Schumann – im Unterschied zur konventionellen Titelbezeichnung „Sonate für Pianoforte und Violine", die er selbst noch für Opus 105 verwandte und die Johannes Brahms und andere Komponisten bis zum Ende des 19. Jahrhunderts gebrauchten – sein Opus 121 als *Sonate für Violine und Pianoforte* bezeichnete. Ob hiermit das Primat des Soloinstrumentes gegenüber dem Pianoforte hervorgehoben und eine neuartige Stellung der beiden Instrumente zueinander betont werden sollte, oder ob vielmehr zwischen der Hervorhebung der Violine im Titel und dem späteren Widmungsträger des Werkes, Ferdinand David,[17] ein Zusammenhang besteht, ist nicht zu klären[18].

Von den Zeitgenossen wurde das Werk zweifellos als neuartig empfunden. Dies belegt beispielsweise die Einschätzung Wasielewskis, dem ersten Interpreten des Werkes:

Diese tiefernste, mit Ausnahme des reizenden langsamen Satzes, düstere Tonschöpfung von heftig aufgeregtem, in den beiden letzten Teilen stürmisch bewegtem Charakter, ist ungleich bedeutender als ihre Vorläuferin. Die darin enthaltenen Schwierigkeiten für beide Instrumente erfordern ein sehr sorgsames Studium, und nicht minder ein liebevolles Eingehen auf den nicht so ohne weiteres wiederzugebenden wuchtigen Gehalt. Das Stück wurde mehrfach probirt, doch mußte ich meine Stimme des Finales wegen allein üben, um damit zurecht zu kommen.[19]

Die nachweislich erste öffentliche Darbietung der Sonate fand am 29. Oktober 1853 im Cürtenschen Saale in Düsseldorf durch Clara Schumann und Joseph Joachim statt.[20] Joachim, der die Sonate Ende August 1853 mit Clara Schumann im Schumannschen Hause gespielt hatte[21], war von dem Werk begeistert und schrieb am 10. September 1853 an Arnold Wehner: *Nicht unterlassen will ich aber, Dich auf die neue Sonate (D moll) aufmerksam zu machen, ... sie ist für mich eine der schönsten Schöpfungen der neuern Zeit, in ihrer herrlichen Einheit der Stimmung und Prägnanz der Motive. Sie ist voll hoher Leidenschaft, – fast herb und schroff in ihren Accenten – und der letzte Satz könnte an eine Seelenlandschaft mahnen in seinem herrlichen Auf- und Niederwogen.*[22] In der Folgezeit ist die 2. Violinsonate öffentlich und im privaten Kreis gespielt worden. Aus der Biographie Litzmanns und der eigenen Programmsammlung Cl. Schumanns sind wiederum vor allem Aufführungen durch sie und J. Joachim überliefert[23]. Letztmalig in Schumanns Beisein ist die Sonate am 23. und 29. Januar 1854 in Hannover gespielt worden[24].

Diese beiden zeitlich unmittelbar nacheinander entstandenen Violinsonaten sind zeitlich versetzt gedruckt worden. Während die erste Sonate bereits Anfang 1852 im Verlag Friedrich Hofmeister erschien, lag der Druck der zweiten Violinsonate erst zu Clara Schumanns Geburtstag am 13. September 1853 vor. Derartige Zeitdifferenzen zwischen Kompositionsabschluss und Drucklegung waren bei Schumann keine Seltenheit. In diesem Falle könnte der Wunsch des Komponisten, kurz nach Erscheinen der ersten Violinsonate im Januar 1852 nicht sogleich ein weiteres Werk dieser Gattung folgen zu lassen, ein Grund dafür gewesen sein. Die Sonate erschien nach vergeblichen Verhandlungen mit den Verlagen Friedrich Hofmeister und Bote & Bock schließlich bei Breitkopf und Härtel in Leipzig. Obwohl der Verlag bereits im Januar 1853 Schumanns Angebot annahm, zögerte sich der Druck bis zum Herbst des Jahres hinaus. Am 10. September schickte der Verlag den fertigen Druck der zweiten Violinsonate zusammen mit den Klavierauszügen des *Manfred* und der vierten Sinfonie nach Düsseldorf, so dass Schumann sie seiner Frau am 13. September 1853 zum Geburtstag überreichen konnte.

Bereits 1854 wurde die Sonate in Frankreich bei Simon Richault herausgegeben. Nach 1860 erschienen eine Bearbeitung für Pianoforte zu 4 Händen von August Horn sowie eine Bearbeitung für Pianoforte und Violoncello von Friedrich Grützmacher.

Ute Bär

1 *Korespondencja Schumanna*, Briefhandschriften in der Bibliotheka Jagiellońska, Kraków, Bd. 21, Nr. 3821, abgedruckt in: Werner Schwarz, *Eine Musikerfreundschaft des 19. Jahrhunderts. Unveröffentlichte Briefe von Ferdinand David an Robert Schumann*, in: *Zum 70. Geburtstag von Joseph Müller-Blattau*, Kassel etc. 1966 (*Saarbrücker Studien zur Musikwissenschaft*, Bd. 1), S. 296–297. David datierte den Brief auf den 18. Januar 1849, wobei er sich in der Jahreszahl irrte. Der Brief ist 1850 geschrieben, was der Hinweis des 1810 geborenen Schreibers am Ende des Briefes: *Morgen werde ich 40 Jahre alt, lieber Schumann*, bestätigt.

2 *Robert Schumann. Projectenbuch*, Robert-Schumann-Haus, Zwickau; Archiv-Nr.: 4871 / VII C, 8 – A3, S. 60.

3 Robert-Schumann-Haus Zwickau, *R. Schumann Handexemplare*, Bd. 18, Archiv-Nr.: 4501, Bd. 18 – D1/A4.

4 *Robert Schumann. Tagebücher*, Bd. III: *Haushaltbücher 1837–1856*, hg. v. Gerd Nauhaus, Basel, Frankfurt [2] [1988] (im Folgenden: *Tb III*), S. 571–572.

5 Berthold Litzmann, *Clara Schumann. Ein Künstlerleben. Nach Tagebüchern und Briefen*, Bd. 2: *Ehejahre 1840–1856*, Leipzig [2]1906 (im Folgenden: *Litzmann II*), S. 264–265.

6 Wilhelm Joseph von Wasielewski, *Aus siebzig Jahren*, Leipzig 1897, S. 125.

7 Zu den Quellenbeschreibungen der 1. und 2. Violinsonate vgl. *Robert Schumann. Neue Ausgabe sämtlicher Werke*, Serie II, Werkgruppe 2, Bd. 3, *Violinsonaten*, hg. v. Ute Bär, Mainz 2001 (im Folgenden: *RSA II/2/3*).

8 Vgl. u. a. *Tb III*; *Ruppert Becker. Tagebuchnotizen*, Robert-Schumann-Haus Zwickau, Archiv-Nr.: 4680 – A3 (unveröffentlicht) sowie *Litzmann II*.

9 Vgl. *Clara Schumann. Programm-Sammlung*, Robert Schumann-Haus Zwickau, Archiv-Nr.: 10463 – C3/A3/A4.

10 Über die Vorbereitung der Konzerte gibt der Briefwechsel beider Künstler Auskunft, der teilweise abgedruckt ist in: Andreas Moser, *Joseph Joachim. Ein Lebensbild*, Bd. I/II, Berlin 1906 und *Briefe von und an Joseph Joachim*, hg. von Johannes Joachim und Andreas Moser, Bd. I–III, Berlin 1911–1913. Weitere, bisher unveröffentlichte Briefe Clara Schumanns befinden sich im Robert-Schumann-Haus, Zwickau.

11 *Neue Zeitschrift für Musik*, Bd. 37, Nr. 12, 17. September 1852, S. 117–120.

12 *Calculations-Buch* des Verlages Friedrich Hofmeister: Sächsisches Staatsarchiv Leipzig; Sign.: Musikverlag Hofmeister Nr. 44.

13 *Tb III*, S. 575–576.

14 *Litzmann II*, S. 265.

15 Vgl. Wilhelm Joseph von Wasielewski, *Schumanniana*, Bonn 1883, S. 31–32.

16 *Litzmann II*, S. 265–266.

17 Schumann hat die Widmung an David als soggetto cavato in den 1. Satz des viersätzigen Werkes einkomponiert. Das Hauptthema wird mit den Tönen *D-A-F-D* eröffnet (T. 21–22), wobei der Ton *F* für den musikalisch nicht darstellbaren Buchstaben V steht. Ein musikalischer Hinweis auf den Widmungsträger ist aber bereits in der langsamen Einleitung zu finden: In den obersten Tönen der ersten 4. Akkorde der Violine wird das in T. 21 beginnende Hauptthema mit der Tonfolge *D-A-F-D* vorweggenommen.

18 Auch für Schumann und seine Zeitgenossen scheint diese Titelgebung neuartig gewesen zu sein. Der Komponist selbst schwankte bei Titelangaben zu dieser Sonate und verwendete verschiedentlich auch noch die traditionelle Formulierung.

19 Wasielewski, *Aus siebzig Jahren*, S. 126

20 Vgl. Theodor Müller-Reuter, *Lexikon der deutschen Konzertliteratur*, Leipzig 1909, S. 191–192.

[21] Joseph Joachim weilte vom 28. August bis 1. September 1853 bei den Schumanns in Düsseldorf. In dieser Zeit wurde verschiedentlich musiziert. Wann genau die 2. Violinsonate gespielt worden ist, geht aus den Hinweisen Schumanns ebensowenig wie aus den überlieferten Tagebuchaufzeichnungen Claras hervor.

[22] *Briefe von und an Joseph Joachim,* Bd. 1: *Die Jahre 1842–1857*, Berlin 1911, S. 74.

[23] Vgl. *Clara Schumann. Programm-Sammlung.*

[24] Vgl. Robert Schumann, *Tagebücher*, Bd. II: *1836–1854*, hg. v. Gerd Nauhaus, Leipzig 1987, S. 448–449 und *Litzmann II*, S. 292.

HINWEISE ZUR INTERPRETATION

Klavier

Robert Schumanns Werke für das Duo Klavier / Violine gehören zu den bedeutendsten Schöpfungen dieser Gattung im 19. Jahrhundert. Zu Beginn seiner Tätigkeit in Düsseldorf schrieb er 1851 die beiden ersten Sonaten; sie stehen in den Tonarten a-Moll und d-Moll, die er in seinen späteren Jahren bevorzugte. Typisch für den großen Romantiker ist die Spielanweisung zum ersten Satz von Opus 105: *Mit leidenschaftlichem Ausdruck*. In seinem immer noch weit unterschätzten Spätwerk ist zudem eine lange und intensive Beschäftigung mit dem Schaffen von Bach zu erkennen, die zu einer Art romantischer Polyphonie führte. Charakteristisch für den späten Schumann ist zudem die Arbeit mit musikalischen Keimzellen, aus denen er das Tonmaterial ganzer Kompositionen ableitete; er hatte solche Techniken in Beethovens letzten Werken gefunden und weiterentwickelt.

Nur in Opus 121 hat der Komponist für wenige Noten im Klavierpart eine Applikatur angegeben; diese wurde durch Kursivdruck gekennzeichnet. Als Angebot an potentielle Spieler wurden an problematischen Stellen Fingersätze hinzugefügt, die darauf angelegt sind, dem Schumannschen Klaviersatz gerecht zu werden; sie offerieren u.a. Möglichkeiten zum Legatospiel, – auch durch Fingerwechsel. Ein ungewöhnlicher Fingersatz wie z. B. der in Opus 105, zweiter Satz, Takt 75 soll ermöglichen, das kurze Motiv in der Basslage wirklich *pianissimo* zu interpretieren.

Schumann hat aber mehrfach indirekte Fingersätze angegeben, durch die er die Verteilung auf die Hände regelt: In Opus 105, erster Satz, Takt 102 schreibt er an die beiden letzten Noten des oberen Systems *Linke*, im letzten Satz derselben Sonate, Takt 117 *Rechte* an zwei Noten des unteren Systems. Gelegentlich zeigt er die Aufteilung durch eine senkrechte Klammer an, wie z. B. im letzten Satz von Opus 105, Takt 13. Solche Arrangements, Umverteilungen von Noten von einem System auf das andere, waren damals schon bekannt.

Gern nutzt Schumann den sonoren Klang der unteren Mittellage des Klaviers als Register; aus praktischen Gründen notiert er dann, wie z. B. am Beginn des ersten Satzes von Opus 105, Noten, die der rechten Hand zugedacht sind, teilweise im Bassschlüssel. In diesem Beispiel ist es selbstverständlich, dass die rechte Hand alle Sechzehntel übernehmen muss, auch die im unteren System. – An komplexer angelegten Stellen wurden Möglichkeiten zur Umverteilung, die sich vielleicht nicht automatisch erschließen, durch den Fingersatz angedeutet; zur Vermeidung von Unklarheiten wurden gelegentlich Häkchen eingefügt.

Besondere Sorgfalt hat Schumann den Basslinien gewidmet. Diese bilden nicht nur das Fundament für die Harmonik, sondern sind Bestandteil einer linear komponierten Melodik. Die eigenständige Führung des Basses ist selbst an Stellen zu konstatieren, an denen ein Zusammenhang mit anderem thematischen Material nicht auf den ersten Blick erkennbar ist. Unter diesem Aspekt wird die Ausführung weitgespannter Griffe, wie Schumann sie besonders der linken Hand zumutet, zu einem echten Problem. Am Beginn der zweiten Sonate z. B. sind die Basstöne nicht nur Pendant zur Oberstimme, sondern vielmehr wesentliches Bauelement des Satzes. Sie sollten gleichzeitig mit der Oberstimme (bzw. der rechten Hand) angeschlagen werden, damit sie mittels sauberen Pedalspiels ihrer Bedeutung entsprechend klingen können. Kaum ein Pianist wird hier ohne Akkordbrechungen auskommen, und somit wäre ein schnelles Arpeggio, mit der Bassnote auf dem Schlag, denkbar. Da Schumann aber normalerweise Klavierakkorde, die er arpeggieren will, mit einem Arpeggio-Symbol bezeichnet, sollte erwogen werden, wenigstens die jeweils unteren Akkordtöne auf dem Schlag zu spielen, den oberen Ton sofort danach.

Ein weiteres Problem bilden die klein gedruckten Vorschlagsnoten in tiefer Lage. Sie sind bei Schumann durchweg nicht als Nebensächlichkeit zu verstehen, sondern als vollgültige und gewichtige Bestandteile des Satzes, oft als Fundament für die Harmonik. Man kann davon ausgehen, dass Vorschlagsnoten seit dem späteren 18. Jahrhundert zunehmend vor dem Schlag genommen wurden. Spieler sollten nachdenken, inwieweit diese in den Hauptakkord integriert werden müssen bzw. können. Eine Stelle sei zumindest erwähnt, an der es unumgänglich scheint, sie mit dem jeweils folgenden Akkord unter einem Pedal zu vereinen, obwohl die Notation dem nicht entspricht: In Opus 105, erster Satz, Takt 206–209 wird die kadenzierende Basslinie von *C* über die klein gedruckten Noten *D* und *E* zum $\underline{A}$ geführt. Der Satz würde ohne den Grundton $\underline{A}$ auf dem Quartsextakkord der Tonika schließen.

An manchen Stellen hat Schumann seine Vorstellung von Pedalspiel mit den üblichen Zeichen dargestellt, gelegentlich aber durch die eher allgemein gehaltene Bemerkung *mit Pedal*. Seine Angaben besitzen exemplarischen Charakter und geben wertvolle Hinweise. Es ist aber zu bedenken, dass zu Schumanns Zeit der Klavierklang noch nicht so voluminös war wie der heutiger Instrumente; zudem war der Nachklang weniger stark und verhallte früher.

Das Pedal kann und sollte selbstverständlich auch dann benutzt werden, wenn der Komponist es nicht ausdrücklich vorgeschrieben hat. Es muss aber die Maxime gelten, dass dessen Einsatz an den Charakter des jeweiligen Stücks gebunden ist sowie an den Verlauf von Harmonik und Melodik; die Klarheit der linearen Stimmführung darf nicht beeinträchtigt werden.

Pedalspiel bedeutet ferner nicht automatisch, dass der Hebel ganz nach unten bewegt und arretiert wird, vielmehr sind große Variabilität und Anschlagskultur nötig. Manchmal ist eine Art Pedalvibrato hilfreich, besonders, wenn im Decrescendo der Klang abgebaut werden soll, wie in Opus 121, erster Satz, Takt 109–110 sowie an Parallelstellen. Ein besonderer Nachhalleffekt findet sich in Opus 105, zweiter Satz, Takt 48–50, wo Schumann verschiedene Harmonien mittels Pedalspiel übereinander geschichtet hat. Natürlich darf auf solche – gelegentlich schon bei Beethoven auftretenden – Klangmischungen, für die eine sehr subtile Pedalkultur nötig ist, nicht verzichtet werden. In Opus 121, erster Satz, Takt 71 wurde für die erste Bassoktave ein Kompromissfingersatz vorgeschlagen, der einen Pedalwechsel auf dem zweiten Viertel ermöglicht, ohne dass das Fundament verloren geht. Schumanns Bezeichnung *mit Ped.* erlaubt diese Lösung. Derselbe Fingersatz sollte für Parallelstellen gelten, selbst wenn in Takt 239 die Pedalangabe, vielleicht irrtümlich, davon abweicht. In Opus 121, erster Satz, Takt 6ff. und Takt 20 – wie auch an anderen Stellen – zeigt der Komponist, dass das Pedal über die eingezeichneten Pausen hinweg arretiert werden soll.

Das linke Pedal (*una corda*) setzt Schumann im dritten Satz von Opus 121 zeitweilig ein, gleichsam als Register bzw. neue Klangfarbe. Er benutzt dazu die Wendungen *mit Verschiebung* und *ohne Verschiebung*.

Jeder Spieler sollte sein Pedalspiel nicht nur gut durchdenken, sondern ständig mit kritischem Gehör überprüfen. Er wird dann zu variabler Gestaltung fähig sein und sich den jeweiligen Gegebenheiten von Instrument und Raum anpassen können.

Der Beginn des ersten Satzes von Opus 121 verweist anagrammatisch auf den Widmungsträger, den mit Schumann befreundeten Geiger Ferdinand David. Der Komponist hat die musikalisch umsetzbaren Buchstaben des Nachnamens als Themenkopf verwendet, wobei er das *v* durch ein *f* ersetzte: *d''- a'-f''-d''*. Diese Töne bilden – bei Oktavierung des zweiten – zugleich den Themenkopf von Bachs *Die Kunst der Fuge*. Der Charakter von Schumanns *ziemlich langsamer* Einleitung mag zudem, nicht zuletzt durch den Rhythmus im dritten Takt, an Bachs berühmte *Chaconne* d-Moll aus der Partita II für Violine solo BWV 1004 erinnern.

Peter Roggenkamp

Violine

Das Bedürfnis, den spezifischen Schumann-Klang wirklich hörbar zu machen, ist der Hauptgrund für die zuweilen etwas unorthodoxen Fingersätze und Bogen-Aufteilungen.

Schumann hatte eine ausgeprägte Vorliebe für die Mittel-Lage der Violine. Diese Lage produziert die wärmsten Klänge, nie aber brillante oder wirklich laute Töne. Gleichzeitig ist der Klaviersatz, besonders in Opus 121, ziemlich dicht und der moderne Flügel voluminöser im Ton als die Instrumente der Schumann-Zeit. Will man also eine ausgewogene Partnerschaft zwischen der Violine und dem (modernen) Klavier, sollte man so viel Bogen wie möglich benutzen und eben auch den Bogen trennen. Voraussetzung ist allerdings eine geschmeidige Bogentechnik sowie das Bewusstsein für die originale Bogeneinteilung. Sehr oft, schon in Beethovens Sonate op. 30 Nr. 1 (erster Satz), sind die Bögen als Phrasierungs-Anweisung zu verstehen und nicht nur als bogentechnische Vorschriften. Als Phrasierungszeichen sind sie unbedingt zu beachten.

Eine Bogentechnische Besonderheit ist für den letzten Satz der Sonate op. 105 von Bedeutung. Es gibt einen deutlichen Unterschied zwischen *non legato* (der ganze Anfang) und *spiccato*. *Spiccato* sind nur die Passagen zu spielen, die auch entsprechend gekennzeichnet sind, also . Alle anderen Sechzehntel sollten kurz, möglichst in der oberen Hälfte des Bogens gespielt werden, mit einem leichten, etwas von der Saite abgehobenen *détaché*. Auf diese Weise werden die wirklichen *Spiccato*-Stellen viel markanter, sogar etwas „unheimlicher" (im *pianissimo*), während die übrigen Sechzehntel besser mit denen des Klaviers zusammenklingen.

Christiane Edinger

PREFACE

Robert Schumann, whose works were characterized by the fact that he produced several works of the same genre in direct sequence, increasingly turned towards composing chamber music in the autumn of 1851, at the end of his first year in Düsseldorf. Between September 12 and November 2, he subsequently composed his first two violin sonatas Op. 105 A minor and Op. 121 D minor, interrupted by his Piano Trio Op. 110 in G minor.

He was probably inspired to compose his first violin sonata by a letter by Gewandhaus concertmaster Ferdinand David, who wrote to him on January 18, 1850 as follows: 'I like your *Fantasy Pieces* for piano and clarinet very much indeed. Why is it that you don't write anything for violin and piano? There is such a shortage of well-written new works and I can't think of anybody who could do it better than you. How nice it would be, if you were to write something of that sort now, that I could then play to you with your wife.'[1]

Schumann did not immediately comply with this request, as his first violin sonata Op. 105 was not composed until September of 1851. Apart from the notes in his *Projectenbuch*[2] and the flyleaf of his personal copy of the original edition[3], Schumann's *Haushaltbuch* provides detailed information about the genesis of this work:

September 12, 1851	Duo for piano and violin
September 14, 1851	For piano and violin
September 15, 1851	More or less finished Violin Sonata
September 16, 1851	Worked hard – finished Sonata.[4]

Only a few days after the completion of the work, Clara Schumann learned the new piece, but the first private performance Clara had been looking forward so much did not take place until October 16, after the return of Wilhelm Joseph von Wasielewski, who was concertmaster of the *Allgemeiner Musikverein* in Düsseldorf from 1850 through 1852. She wrote the following about the performance: 'I was so restless, I had to try Robert's new sonata this very day. We played it, and were particularly moved by the very elegiac first movement and the lovely second movement. Only the somewhat less charming, more unyielding third movement caused us some difficulty.'[5] And Wasielewski commented: 'On the whole Schumann was satisfied with the performance, only my playing of the Finale failed to please him. We went through it three more times, but Schumann said that he had expected the violin part to have a different effect. I was unable to convey the unyielding, brusque tone of the piece to his satisfaction.'[6]

Therefore the historical sources for this sonata, the autograph and the original editions of the piano score and the violin part from 1852 also show numerous differences, particularly in this case, indicating corrections that must have been made to the engraver's copy missing today.[7] The numerous changes illustrate that the finale had originally not met Schumann's expectations.

Following a performance on March 9 for Prince Reuß, the first public performance finally took place on March 21 at the Leipzig Gewandhaus. Any other public performances at the time of Schumann are not known, which does not come as a surprise, since according to the 19th century appreciation, the violin sonata belonged to the category of demanding private chamber music. The composition was performed in this context, as is verified by various sources.[8] Following Schumann's death, mainly interpretations by Clara Schumann and Joseph Joachim[9] became known – both from her historic diary entries as well as her own program collection[10].

The negative review by Wagnerian Theodor Uhlig (1822–1853) in the *Neue Zeitschrift für Musik* dated September 17, 1852, stands diametrically contradictory to estimates made by Schumann's personal environment, describing Schumann a mannerist and extensive writer and accusing him of a lack in originality.[11] This judgement was not able to damage the publicity and distribution of this composition that was published at the beginning of 1852 by the Leipzig publisher Friedrich Hofmeister, as the sales figures of the publisher's account book will verify[12]. The various editions published after 1860 speak for an appreciation of this work.

Just a few weeks after his first violin sonata, Schumann composed his second violin sonata between October 26 and November 2. Once again, Schumann's *Haushaltbuch* provides detailed information about the composition of this work:

October 28, 1851:	Scherzo of the 2nd sonata for violin [2nd movement]
October 29, 1851:	Andante of the 2nd sonata. [3rd movement]
November 2, 1851:	2nd sonata more or less finished.[13]

However, on November 4, 1851, Clara Schumann still wrote in her diary: 'Robert is industriously working on a second sonata for piano and violin. I await it with burning impatience.'[14] It may thus be assumed that at first, the composition was merely sketched down in a working manuscript by November 2 and not finalized until the next couple of days. The first private performance by Clara Schumann and Wilhelm Joseph von Wasielewski took place on November 15, 1851 in Düsseldorf. Schumann must therefore have finalized and copied this sonata between November 4 and 15, as a performance from the autograph would not have been possible due to numerous deletions, corrections and omissions of complete sections made on the working manuscript. The copy used for this private performance was the engraver's copy and the fair copy of the violin part. The corrections Schumann made to the first movement according to Wasielewski, as contained in this piano score[15] copy verify this.

Regarding the new composition, Clara Schumann made the following entry in her diary on November 15, 1851: 'It is another work of wonderful originality with a profundity and grandeur such I have scarcely ever encountered – it really is utterly overwhelming music.'[16] She sounded just as excited in her letters to her mother Mariane Bargiel and the friend of the family by the name of Avé Lallemant.

After finalizing his first violin sonata, Schumann composed the second work of this genre just about a month later. Schumann's comment on the reason for composing a second work '... I didn't like the first violin sonata; so I wrote a second one, which I hope has turned out better' certainly is to be more regarded from an ironic point of view against himself and less as an expression of total dissatisfaction; otherwise Schumann would certainly not have published his first sonata in print already in January of 1852. The composition title, *Zweite grosse Sonate für Violine und Pianoforte* employs the attribute *grosse* ['large'] to emphasize the fact that they are classified differently. In this context it is interesting that Schumann – opposed to the conventional title 'Sonata for Piano and Violin' that he still used for Opus 105 and that Johannes Brahms as well as other composers kept using until the end of the 19th century – he entitled his Opus 121

'Sonata for Violin and Piano'. Whether he meant to emphasize the primacy of the solo instrument with regard to the piano this way, distinguishing a new type of relation between the two instruments or whether a connection exists between the accentuation of the violin as part of the title and Ferdinand David[17] to whom the work was later dedicated to, remains open.

There is no doubt that his contemporaries considered this composition a novelty. For example, this is verified by Wasielewski's interpretation, the first performer of this work: 'This profoundly serious and, except for the charming slow movement, dark piece of music with its violently agitated tempestuous character in the last two parts, is incomparably more significant than its predecessor. The difficulties which it presents for both instruments necessitate very careful study, and, no less, loving attention to the powerful content, which is not at all easy to convey. The piece was rehearsed a number of times, but I had to rehearse my part alone in order to be able to cope with the Finale.'[18]

This sonata was first verifiably performed in public on October 29, 1853 at Cürten hall in Düsseldorf by Clara Schumann and Joseph Joachim.[19] Joachim who had played the sonata at the end of August of 1853 together with Clara Schumann at Schumann's home was fascinated by the work, and on September 10, 1853, he wrote to Arnold Wehner: 'But I must not omit to draw your attention to the new sonata (D minor) ... For me it is one of the most beautiful works of recent times with its splendid unity of mood and the conciseness of its themes. It is full of lofty passion, – with an almost astringent, brusque tone – and the last movement with its splendid surging flow, could make one think of a landscape of the soul.'[20] After the first performance, the second violin sonata was performed in public and private circles. From Litzmann's biography and Cl. Schumann's own program collection, on the other hand, mainly performances by her and J. Joachim have become known.[21] In the presence of Schumann, the sonata was performed for the last time on January 23 and 29, 1854 in Hannover.[22]

These two violin sonatas that were composed right after one another were printed with a lapse in time. While the first sonata had already been published by Friedrich Hofmeister at the beginning of 1852, the print of the second sonata was not finished until September 13, 1853, the birthday of Clara Schumann. Such time lapses between the completion of the work and its printing was not unusual for Schumann. Possibly in this case, the composer not wanting to publish yet another work of this genre right after the first violin sonata was published in January of 1852 could have been a reason. After futile negotiations with the Friedrich Hofmeister and Bote & Bock Publishing Companies, the sonata was finally published by Breitkopf und Härtel in Leipzig. Although the publisher had already accepted Schumann's proposal by January of 1853, the score print was delayed until the autumn of that year. On September 10, the publisher sent the completed print together with piano score of *Manfred* and the fourth symphony to Düsseldorf so that Schumann could present them to his wife on her birthday on September 13, 1853.

The sonata was already published in France by Simon Richault as early as 1854. After 1860, an edition for piano duet by August Horn as well as an edition for piano and cello by Friedrich Grützmacher were published.

Ute Bär
(Translation Peggy Möller)

1 *Korespondencja Schumanna*, manuscript letters in the Bibliotheka Jagiellońska, Kraków, Vol. 21, No. 3821, published in: Werner Schwarz, 'Eine Musikerfreundschaft des 19. Jahrhunderts. Unveröffentlichte Briefe von Ferdinand David an Robert Schumann', in: *Zum 70. Geburtstag von Joseph Müller-Blattau,* Kassel etc., 1966 (*Saarbrücker Studien zur Musikwissenschaft,* Vol. 1), pp. 296–297. David dated the letter to January 18, 1849, making a mistake with regard to the year. The letter was written in 1850, confirmed by the note by the writer born in 1810 put at the end of this letter: 'I shall be 40 tomorrow, dear Schumann.'

2 *Robert Schumann. Projectenbuch*, Robert-Schumann-Haus, Zwickau; archive no.: 4871 / VII C, 8 – A3, p. 60.

3 Robert-Schumann-Haus Zwickau, *R. Schumann Handexemplare*, Vol. 18, archive no.: 4501, Vol. 18 – D1/A4.

4 *Robert Schumann. Tagebücher*, Vol. III: *Haushaltbücher 1837–1856*, ed. by Gerd Nauhaus, Basle, Frankfurt, [2] [1988] (in the following: *Tb III*), pp. 571–572.

5 Berthold Litzmann, *Clara Schumann. Ein Künstlerleben. Nach Tagebüchern und Briefen*, Vol. 2: *Ehejahre 1840–1856,* Leipzig, [2]1906 (in the following: *Litzmann II*), pp. 264–265.

6 Wilhelm Joseph von Wasielewski, *Aus siebzig Jahren*, Leipzig, 1897, p. 125.

7 On the sources of the 1st and 2nd violin sonatas see *Robert Schumann. Neue Ausgabe sämtlicher Werke*, Series II, Group 2, Vol. 3, *Violinsonaten*, ed. by Ute Bär, Mainz 2001 (in the following: *RSA II/2/3*).

8 Cf. among others *Tb III*; *Ruppert Becker. Tagebuchnotizen*, Robert-Schumann-Haus Zwickau, archive no.: 4680 – A3 (unpublished) and *Litzmann II*.

9 Cf. Andreas Moser, *Joseph Joachim. Ein Lebensbild,* Vol. I/II, Berlin 1906 and *Briefe von und an Joseph Joachim*, ed. by Johannes Joachim and Andreas Moser, Vol. I–III, Berlin 1911–1913. Other letters of Clara Schumann that have not been published yet may be found at the Robert-Schumann-Haus, Zwickau.

10 Cf. *Clara Schumann. Programm-Sammlung*, Robert Schumann-Haus Zwickau, archive no.: 10463 – C3/A3/A4.

11 *Neue Zeitschrift für Musik*, Vol. 37, No. 12, September 17, 1852, pp. 117–120.

12 *Calculations-Buch* by the Friedrich Hofmeister Publishing Company: Sächsisches Staatsarchiv Leipzig, Musikverlag Hofmeister Nr. 44.

13 *Tb III*, pp. 575–576.

14 *Litzmann II*, p. 265.

15 Cf. Wilhelm Joseph von Wasielewski, *Schumanniana*, Bonn, 1883, pp. 31–32.

16 *Litzmann II*, pp. 265–266.

17 Schumann incorporated his dedication to David as *soggetto cavato* in the main theme of the 1st movement and in the slow introduction with the notes *D-A-F-D* (bars 21–22), whereas the note *F* represents the letter *V* which cannot be represented as a musical note.

18 Wasielewski, *Aus siebzig Jahren*, p. 126

19 Cf. Theodor Müller-Reuter, *Lexikon der deutschen Konzertliteratur*, Leipzig 1909, pp. 191–192.

20 *Briefe von und an Joseph Joachim,* Vol. 1: *Die Jahre 1842–1857*, Berlin, 1911, p. 74.

21 Cf. *Clara Schumann. Programm-Sammlung*.

22 Cf. *Robert Schumann. Tagebücher*, Vol. II: *1836–1854*, ed. by Gerd Nauhaus, Leipzig, 1987, pp. 448–449 and *Litzmann II*, p. 292.

NOTES ON INTERPRETATION

Piano

Robert Schumann's works for piano and violin are some of the most significant compositions of this genre from the 19th century. At the beginning of his work in Düsseldorf, he wrote his first two sonatas in 1851; they are written in A minor and D minor, the keys he preferred during his later years. The performance instructions provided for the first movement of Opus 105 are characteristic of the great Romanticist: *Mit leidenschaftlichem Ausdruck* ['with passionate expression']. The fact that he intensely dealt with the works of Bach for a long time also becomes evident in his late work that is still by far underestimated, leading to a sort of a Romantic polyphony. Furthermore, his work with musical nuclei from where he derived thematic material for whole compositions is also characteristic of the late Schumann; such techniques he had discovered in Beethoven's last works and continued to develop them.

In the piano part the composer merely indicated fingering in Opus 121 for a few notes; these are printed in italics. As a suggestion to potential performers, fingerings have been added to problematic spots, construed to come up to the Schumannian piano setting; among other things, they provide opportunities for playing legato, also through changing fingers. An unusual fingering, such as in Opus 105, second movement, bar 75, for example, is supposed to enable the performer to really interpret the short motive in the bass range as a *pianissimo*.

However, Schumann repeatedly indicated indirect fingerings in his arrangement of the hands: In Opus 105, first movement, bar 102, he marked the two final notes of the upper system *Linke* ['left hand'], and during the final movement of that same sonata, bar 117, he marked two notes of the lower system *Rechte* ['right hand']. He occasionally indicates his arangement by a vertical bracket, such as during the final movement of Opus 105, bar 13, for example. Such arrangements, shifting notes from one system to another, were already known at that time.

Schumann likes to make use of the sonorous sound of the lower medium range of the piano as a register; at the beginning of the first movement of Opus 105, for example, for practical reasons he partially arranges notes intended for the right hand in bass clef. This example certainly shows that the right hand has to take over all sixteenth notes, including the ones in the lower system. – More complex spots that might not automatically become clear were equipped with options to shift; in order to avoid ambiguities, checkmarks have been added occasionally.

Schumann payed special attention to the bass lines. These do not only lay the foundation for the harmonic line, they are also part of a linearly composed melodic line. The independent direction of the bass may even be ascertained in spots where the context to other thematic material may not be perceived at first sight. With this in mind, the performance of wide chords, such as Schumann especially expects of the left hand, becomes a real problem. At the beginning of the second sonata, for example, the bass notes are not only a counterpart to the upper part, but rather a significant component of the setting. They should be played together with the upper part (or the right hand, respectively) at the same time in order for them to sound accordingly while employing clean pedaling techniques. Hardly any pianist will be able to get by without breaking the chords and a rapid arpeggio with the bass note played on the beat might seem plausible. However, since Schumann usually marked piano chords that he wants to see arpeggiated with an arpeggio symbol, the performer should consider playing the respective lower chord tones on the beat, right away followed by the upper tone.

Another problem is brought up by the low-range grace notes in small print. In Schumann's works they are not to be considered secondary at all, but rather as full and important part of the movement, often laying the foundation for the harmonic line. It may be assumed that during the later part of the 18th century, appoggiaturas were increasingly played before the beat. Performers should consider how far they may or must be integrated into the main chord. At least one place should be mentioned, where it seems inevitable to combine it with the subsequent chord under the same pedal position, even though the notation does not correspond to that: in Opus 105, first movement, bars 206–209, the cadencing bass line goes from *C* to the small-print notes *D* and *E* to *A*. The movement would close without the tonic note *A* on the second inversion of the tonic.

In some instances Schumann illustrated his concept of pedaling with the usual symbols, however, sometimes he used the general remark *mit Pedal* ['with pedal']. His specifications exhibit an examplary character and are useful hints. It must be considered, however, that compared to the sound of our instruments today, the piano sound had not been so powerful yet during the time of Schumann; the reverberation was also less powerful and faded sooner.

The pedal may and also should certainly be used in parts the composer did not specifically mark. However, the performer should follow the guideline that the use of the pedal is bound to the character of each respective piece and on the harmonic and melodic lines; the clarity of the linear voices must not be compromised.

Furthermore, pedaling does not automatically mean that the pedal is moved all the way to the bottom and held down, but rather a high variablility is needed as well as a sense for what is appropriate. Sometimes a sort of a pedal vibrato may be helpful, particularly when a *decrescendo* is calling for a decrease in sound, such as in Opus 121, first movement, bars 109 and 110 and in parallel instances. A special reverberation effect is found in Opus 105, second movement, bars 48–50, where Schumann combined several harmonies by pedaling. These sound combinations – that occasionally made an appearance in the music of Beethoven – may certainly not be foregone; they require a subtle feeling for the use of the pedal. In Opus 121, first movement, bar 71, a compromise solution was suggested for the fingering of the first bass octave, facilitating a change in pedaling during the second quarter without giving up the foundation. Schumann's term *mit Ped.* permits this solution. The same fingering should be applied to parallel passages, even if the pedaling marks, maybe by mistake, deviate from that in bar 239. In Opus 121, first movement, bars 6 sqq. and bar 20 – just like in other instances as well – the composer illustrates that the pedal should be held down through the rests.

Schumann partly uses the left (soft) pedal (*una corda*) in the third movement of Opus 121, as register and new timbre at the same time. In that, he uses the terms *mit Verschiebung* ['with left pedal'] and *ohne Verschiebung* ['without left pedal'].

Each performer should not only consider his use of pedaling very carefully, but he should also listen constantly and critically. He will then be able to perform in a variable manner and adjust to the given circumstances surrounding the instrument and the room.

The beginning of the first movement of Opus 121 anagrammatically refers to the friend Schumann dedicated his work to, the violinist Ferdinand David. The composer incorporated the letters of his last name that may be musically transcribed, replacing the *v* by an *f*: *d″- a′- f″-d″*. These notes also form the beginning of the theme of Bach's 'The Art of Fugue' – by octavization of the second. The character of Schumann's 'fairly slow' introduction (*Ziemlich langsam*) may also remind the listener of Bach's famous 'Chaconne' in D minor from Partita II for Solo Violin BWV 1004, last but not least because of the rhythm incorporated during the third bar.

Peter Roggenkamp
(Translation Peggy Möller)

Violin

The need to make the special Schumann sound really audible is the main reason for the sometimes rather unorthodox fingerings and bowing patterns.

Schumann had a distinct preference for the middle register of the violin. This register produces the warmest sounds, but never brilliant or really loud tones. At the same time, the piano writing, particularly in Opus 121, is rather dense, and the modern grand piano more voluminous in tone than the instruments of Schumann's time. Thus, if a balanced partnership between the violin and the (modern) piano is desired, as much bow should be used as possible, and the bow even detached. Prerequisites for this, however, are a flexible bowing technique and an awareness of the original disposition of the bowing. Very often, even as early as Beethoven's Sonata Op. 30 No. 1 (first movement), the slurs are to be understood as phrasing indications and not only as technical bowing prescriptions. As phrasing marks, they should certainly be taken account of.

A special feature of bowing technique is significant in the last movement of the Sonata Op. 105. There is a clear differentiation between *non legato* (the whole of the beginning) and *spiccato*. Only those passages should be played *spiccato* which are marked as such, thus. All other semiquavers should be played short, as far as possible in the upper half of the bow, with a light *détaché*, somewhat lifted from the string. In this way, the real *spiccato* passages are much more striking, even somewhat 'unearthly' (in the *pianissimo*), while the remaining semiquavers combine much better with those of the piano.

Christiane Edinger
(Translation Peggy Möller)

PRÉFACE

Robert Schumann composait généralement plusieurs œuvres de même genre directement l'une après l'autre, c'est là ce qui caractérisait sa création. En automne 1851, vers la fin de sa première année à Düsseldorf, il s'est de plus en plus adonné à la musique de chambre.

Du 12 septembre au 2 novembre, il composa successivement, avec tout juste une interruption pour le trio pour piano op. 110 en sol mineur, ses deux premières sonates pour violon op. 105 en la mineur et op. 121 en ré mineur.

C'est probablement une lettre du maître de concert de l'orchestre du *Gewandhaus*, Ferdinand David, qui l'incita à composer les premières sonates pour violon, il lui avait écrit le 18 janvier 1850: «Tes fantaisies pour piano et clarinette me plaisent énormément; pourquoi ne fais tu rien pour violon et piano ? Il y a une telle carence en nouveautés pertinentes et je ne connais personne qui le ferait mieux que toi. Comme ce serait bien si tu pouvais composer quelque chose de ce genre, je pourrais ensuite te le jouer accompagné de ta femme.»[1]

Schumann n'a pas répondu immédiatement à cette requête, car c'est en septembre 1851 que fut composée la première sonate pour violon op. 105. Outre les remarques dans son *Projectenbuch*[2] et sur la feuille précédant son propre exemplaire de la première impression[3], l'agenda de Schumann livre des informations détaillées sur la création de l'œuvre:

12 septembre 1851	Duo pour Pianoforte et violon
14 septembre 1851	pour violon et Pianoforte.
15 septembre 1851	j'ai presque achevé la sonate pour violon
16 septembre 1851	Bien appliqué – terminé la sonate.[4]

Clara Schumann découvrit la nouvelle œuvre quelques jours déjà après sa composition, mais ce n'est qu'après le retour de Wilhelm Joseph von Wasielewski, qui avait été le maître de concert de *l'Allgemeiner Musikverein* de Düsseldorf de 1850 à 1852, que put être exécutée le 16 octobre pour la première fois en privé la nouvelle œuvre, tant attendue par Clara, qui écrit à ce sujet: «Je n'y tenais plus, je devais essayer tout de suite la nouvelle sonate de Robert. Nous l'avons jouée et nous sentions émus, particulièrement par le premier mouvement, très élégiaque, et par le second, si charmant, mais le troisième, moins plaisant, et plutôt récalcitrant, ne se laissait pas vraiment exécuter.»[5] Et Wasielewski relate: «dans l'ensemble, Schumann s'est montré satisfait de l'exécution, mais je n'ai pas pu jouer le finale comme il le souhaitait. Je l'ai recommencé à trois reprises, mais Schumann affirmait qu'il attendait un autre effet de la partie violon. Je n'ai pas réussi à en redonner suffisamment le ton volontaire et abrupt.»[6]

C'est ainsi que les sources de cette sonate qui nous ont été transmises, l'autographe et les versions originales des partitions du piano et de la partie soliste datant de 1852, témoignent précisément dans ce mouvement des nombreuses différences qui révèlent l'existence de corrections devant avoir été effectuées sur l'exemplaire gravé[7] aujourd'hui disparu. L'abondance des modifications est probablement la preuve que le finale devait ne pas avoir entièrement correspondu aux attentes de Schumann.

Après une interprétation le 9 mars devant le Prince Reuß, la première exécution en public eut lieu le 21 mars à la Gewandhaus de Leipzig. D'autres interprétations publiques du vivant de Schumann ne sont pas connues, ce qui surprend à peine, car dans l'esprit du XIXe siècle, la sonate pour violon était considérée comme du domaine de la musique de chambre privée, nettement plus exigeante. C'est dans ce contexte que l'œuvre fut interprétée, ce dont témoignent différentes sources.[8] Après la mort de Schumann, tant les notes du journal intime de Clara Schumann que son propre recueil de programmes[9], font mention de ses propres interprétations et de celles de Joseph Joachim.[10]

La critique négative de Theodor Uhlig (1822–1853), féru de Wagner, dans le *Neue Zeitschrift für Musik* du 17 septembre 1852, dans laquelle il qualifie Schumann de «Maniériste» et de «Gribouilleur» et lui reproche son manque total d'originalité[11] est diamétralement opposée aux estimations émanant de l'entourage personnel de Schumann. Ce jugement n'a pas réussi à nuire à la publicité et à la diffusion de l'œuvre qui a été publiée début 1852 aux Éditions Friedrich Hofmeister à Leipzig, ce que prouvent les chiffres des ventes[12]. Les adaptations publiées après 1860 témoignent elles aussi de la grande estime dont jouissait l'œuvre.

Quelques semaines seulement après la première, Schumann composa sa seconde sonate pour violon entre le 26 octobre et le 2 novembre. Là aussi, l'agenda (*Haushaltbuch*) de Schumann livre des informations détaillées sur la création de l'œuvre:

28 octobre 1851:	Scherzo de la seconde sonate p. violon [2e mouvement]
29 octobre 1851:	Andante de la seconde sonate. [3e mouvement]
2 novembre 1851:	Presque achevé la seconde sonate[13]

Toutefois, Clara Schumann écrit encore le 4 novembre 1851 dans son journal intime: «Robert travaille avec ardeur à une seconde sonate pour piano et violon. Je brûle d'impatience de la découvrir[14]» . Nous supposons donc que dans le manuscrit de travail du 2 novembre, l'œuvre n'a été qu'ébauchée et qu'elle n'a été entièrement achevée que dans les jours suivants. C'est à Düsseldorf que Clara Schumann et Wilhelm Joseph von Wasielewski l'ont exécutée pour la première fois en public le 15 novembre 1851. On suppose donc qu'entre le 4 et le 15 novembre, Schumann doit avoir définitivement achevé et copié la sonate, car au vu des nombreuses ratures, corrections et omissions de passages entiers dans le manuscrit de travail, une exécution n'aurait pas été possible avec l'exemplaire autographe. La copie utilisée pour cette représentation privée est le modèle de gravure et la copie au net de la partie violon. Si l'on en croit Wasielewski, les corrections effectuées par Schumann dans le premier mouvement et qui apparaissent dans cette copie de la partition pour piano[15] en sont la preuve manifeste.

Au sujet de la nouvelle œuvre, Clara Schumann a noté le 15 novembre 1851 dans son journal intime: «... elle est aussi d'une merveilleuse originalité et d'une profondeur et d'une splendeur comme je n'en connais aucune autre – voici une musique véritablement bouleversante. »[16] C'est avec tout autant d'enthousiasme qu'elle s'exprimait dans ses lettres à sa mère, Mariane Bargiel et à l'ami de la famille, Avé Lallemant.

C'est ainsi que Schumann écrivit le deuxième morceau de ce genre environ un mois après avoir achevé la première Sonate pour le violon. La remarque de Schumann sur la cause de la composition du nouveau morceau «... la première Sonate pour le violon ne m'a pas plu; c'est pourquoi j'en ai écrit une deuxième qui je l'espère sera plus réussie», est certainement plutôt ironique et moins à comprendre comme l'expression d'une véritable insatisfaction car sinon, Schumann n'aurait pas fait graver la première Sonate dès janvier 1852. Le titre de l'œuvre à lui seul, *Deuxième grande Sonate pour violon et pianoforte*, indique par l'attribut *grande* que des différences de niveau existent entre les deux compositions. Il est intéressant dans ce contexte que Schumann ait intitulé son opus 121 *Sonate pour violon et pianoforte* – et non pas «Sonate pour pianoforte et violon», titre qu'il avait lui-même encore utilisé pour son opus 105 et que Johannes Brahms et d'autres compositeurs utilisèrent jusqu'à la fin du XIXe siècle. On ignore si l'intention était ici de souligner la primauté de l'instrument soliste sur le pianoforte et de mettre en valeur une relation nouvelle des deux instruments entre eux ou bien s'il existe plutôt un rapport entre la mise en valeur du violon dans le titre et le dédicataire ultérieur de l'œuvre, Ferdinand David[17].

Les contemporains furent très certainement sensibles à la nouveauté de cette œuvre. Ce qu'atteste par exemple le jugement de Wasielewski, l'interprète initial du morceau : «Cette création profondément grave, sombre, à l'exception du charmant mouvement lent, d'un caractère intense et emporté, fougueux et chargé d'émotion dans les deux dernières parties, est d'une toute autre signification que la première. Les difficultés qu'elle contient pour les deux instruments exigent une étude des plus minutieuses et un intérêt non moins grand pour le contenu imposant qui n'est pas facile à rendre. Le morceau fut répété plusieurs fois mais je dus travailler seul ma partie du finale afin d'en venir à bout.»[18]

La première représentation attestée de la Sonate eut lieu le 29 octobre 1853 dans la salle Cürten de Düsseldorf, avec comme interprètes Clara Schumann et Joseph Joachim.[19] Joachim, qui avait joué la Sonate fin août 1853 avec Clara Schumann dans la maison des Schumann, fut enthousiasmé par l'œuvre, écrivant le 10 septembre1853 à Arnold Wehner : «Mais je ne vais pas manquer d'attirer ton attention sur la nouvelle Sonate (ré mineur), ... elle est pour moi l'une des plus belles créations de notre époque récente, dans la magnifique unité de son atmosphère et la concision des motifs. Elle est pleine d'une passion élevée – presque austère et rude dans ses accents – et le dernier mouvement pourrait être l'évocation d'un paysage de l'âme dans son merveilleux mouvement qui s'élance et retombe.»[20] Par la suite, la deuxième Sonate fut jouée en public et en privé. La biographie de Litzmann et le propre recueil de programmes de Cl. Schumann mentionnent surtout quant à eux des représentations où les interprètes sont elle-même et J. Joachim.[21] La Sonate fut jouée pour la dernière fois en présence de Schumann les 23 et 29 janvier 1854 à Hanovre.[22]

Ces deux Sonates pour le violon, écrites directement une après l'autre, furent gravées à des époques différentes. Tandis que la première Sonate parut aux Éditions Friedrich Hofmeister dès le début de l'année 1852, la gravure de la deuxième Sonate ne fut prête que pour l'anniversaire de Clara Schumann, le 13 septembre 1853. De tels laps de temps entre l'achèvement d'une composition et la mise sous presse ne sont pas rares dans le cas de Schumann. Ici, une raison pourrait être le vœu du compositeur de ne pas proposer aussitôt après la parution de la première Sonate pour le violon en janvier 1852 une autre œuvre dans ce même genre. Après avoir négocié sans succès avec les Éditions Friedrich Hofmeister et Bote & Bock, la Sonate parut finalement chez Breitkopf et Härtel à Leipzig. Bien que la maison d'édition eût accepté l'offre de Schumann en janvier 1853, la gravure fut retardée jusqu'à l'automne de la même année. Le 10 septembre, la maison d'édition envoya à Düsseldorf la gravure achevée de la deuxième Sonate pour le violon, avec les réductions pour piano de *Manfred* et de la Symphonie n° 4, de sorte que Schumann put en faire présent à sa femme le 13 septembre 1853 pour son anniversaire.

Dès 1854, la Sonate fut éditée en France chez Simon Richault. Après 1860 parurent un arrangement pour pianoforte à 4 mains d'August Horn ainsi qu'un arrangement pour pianoforte et violoncelle de Friedrich Grützmacher.

Ute Bär
(Traduction Micheline Wiechert)

1 *Korespondencja Schumanna*, lettres en manuscrit dans la Bibliotheka Jagiellońska, Kraków, vol. 21, no. 3821, dans: Werner Schwarz, *Eine Musikerfreundschaft des 19. Jahrhunderts. Unveröffentlichte Briefe von Ferdinand David an Robert Schumann*, dans: *Zum 70. Geburtstag von Joseph Müller-Blattau*, Kassel etc. 1966 (*Saarbrücker Studien zur Musikwissenschaft*, Bd. 1), p. 296–297. David data la lettre du 18 janvier 1849, se trompant d'année. La lettre a été écrite en 1850, ce que confirme à la fin de la lettre la remarque de l'auteur, né en 1810 : «Mon cher Schumann, je vais avoir 40 ans demain».

2 Robert Schumann. *Projectenbuch*, Robert-Schumann-Haus, Zwickau, no. des archives: 4871 / VII C, 8 – A3, p. 60.

3 Robert-Schumann-Haus Zwickau, *R. Schumann Handexemplare*, vol. 18, no. des archives: 4501, Bd. 18 – D1/A4.

4 *Robert Schumann. Tagebücher*, vol. III: Haushaltbücher 1837–1856, éd. par Gerd Nauhaus, Basel, Frankfurt 2 [1988] (dans la suite : *Tb III*), pp. 571–572.

5 Berthold Litzmann, *Clara Schumann. Ein Künstlerleben. Nach Tagebüchern und Briefen*, vol. 2: Ehejahre 1840–1856, Leipzig 21906 (dans la suite : *Litzmann II*), pp. 264–265.

6 Wilhelm Joseph von Wasielewski, *Aus siebzig Jahren*, Leipzig 1897, p. 125.

7 Voir aussi pour les descriptions de sources des Sonates pour le violon 1 et 2 : *Robert Schumann. Neue Ausgabe sämtlicher Werke*, Serie II, Werkgruppe 2, vol. 3, *Violinsonaten*, éd. par Ute Bär, Mainz 2001 (dans la suite : *RSA II/2/3*).

8 Cf. u. a. Tb III; *Ruppert Becker. Tagebuchnotizen*, Robert-Schumann-Haus Zwickau, no. des archives: 4680 – A3 (inédit) ainsi que *Litzmann II*.

9 Cf. *Clara Schumann. Programm-Sammlung*, Robert Schumann-Haus Zwickau, no. des archives: 10463 – C3/A3/A4.

10 Cf. Andreas Moser, *Joseph Joachim. Ein Lebensbild*, vol. I/II, Berlin 1906 et *Briefe von und an Joseph Joachim*, éd. par Johannes Joachim et Andreas Moser, vol. I–III, Berlin 1911–1913.

11 *Neue Zeitschrift für Musik*, vol. 37, no. 12, 17. Septembre 1852, pp. 117–120.

12 *Calculations-Buch* des Éditions Friedrich Hofmeister: Sächsisches Staatsarchiv Leipzig; *Musikverlag Hofmeister Nr. 44*.

13 *Tb III*, pp. 575–576.

14 *Litzmann II*, p. 265.

15 Vgl. Wilhelm Joseph von Wasielewski, *Schumanniana*, Bonn 1883, pp. 31–32.

16 *Litzmann II*, pp. 265–266.

17 Schumann a intégré dans la composition la dédicace à David en tant que *soggetto cavato* dans le 1er mouvement de l'œuvre en quatre parties. Le thème principal s'ouvre sur les tons *D-A-F-D* (*ré-la-fa-ré*, mes. 21–22), le ton de *F* (*fa*) symbolisant en musique la lettre *V* non représentable.

18 Wasielewski, *Aus siebzig Jahren*, p. 126

19 Cf. aussi Theodor Müller-Reuter, *Lexikon der deutschen Konzertliteratur*, Leipzig 1909, pp. 191–192.

20 *Briefe von und an Joseph Joachim*, vol. 1: *Die Jahre 1842–1857*, Berlin 1911, p. 74.

21 Cf. aussi *Clara Schumann. Programm-Sammlung*.

22 Cf. Robert Schumann. *Tagebücher*, vol. II : *1836–1854*, éd. par Gerd Nauhaus, Leipzig 1987, pp. 448–449 et *Litzmann II*, p. 292.

NOTES SUR L'INTERPRÉTATION

Piano

Les duos de Robert Schumann pour piano et violon comptent parmi les plus représentatifs du genre au XIXe siècle. Les deux premières sonates en la mineur et en ré mineur, tonalités qu'il privilégiera à la fin de sa vie, remontent à l'année 1851, c'est-à-dire au début de sa carrière à Düsseldorf. L'indication de jeu *avec une expression passionnée* du premier mouvement de l'Opus 105 est révélatrice du grand romantique. Dans son œuvre tardive, encore sous-estimée, on ne peut ignorer l'étude intensive des œuvres de Bach, aboutissant à une sorte de polyphonie romantique. Caractéristique pour l'œuvre de la maturité, Schumann tire à partir de germes musicaux le matériau tonal qu'il applique à des compositions entières, développant une technique qu'il avait découverte dans les œuvres tardives de Beethoven.

Pour l'Opus 121 seulement, et uniquement pour quelques notes de la partie de piano, le compositeur donne des précisions de doigté, imprimées en italiques. À cela s'ajoutent aux endroits problématiques pour l'interprète des propositions de doigté qui lui permettent de respecter l'esprit schumannien. Ces suggestions offrent notamment des possibilités de legato, par exemple en changeant de doigt. Un doigté inhabituel, notamment à la mesure 75 du second mouvement de l'Opus 105, permet de jouer vraiment *pianissimo* le bref motif de la main gauche.

En revanche, Schumann donne indirectement des précisions en indiquant la répartition entre les mains : dans le premier mouvement de l'Opus 105, à la mesure 102, il indique *Linke* [«main gauche»] pour les deux dernières notes de la portée supérieure ; sur deux notes de la portée inférieure, à la mesure 117 du dernier mouvement de la même sonate, il indique *Rechte* [«main droite»]. Par moment, il signale le partage des mains par une accolade verticale, par exemple au dernier mouvement de l'Opus 105, mesure 13. De tels arrangements pour transférer des notes d'une portée vers l'autre étaient déjà en usage à l'époque.

Schumann utilise volontiers la pâte sonore du milieu de la partie basse du clavier comme registre de base ; dans ce cas, pour des raisons pratiques, il écrit parfois à la clé de basse des notes prévues à la main droite, comme au début du premier mouvement de l'Opus 105. Dans cet exemple, il est évident que la main droite doit prendre toutes les doubles croches y comprises celles de la portée inférieure. – A des endroits plus complexes, des possibilités de changement qui ne sont pas immédiatement compréhensibles sont suggérées par le doigté; parfois des petits crochets sont ajoutés pour faciliter la lecture.

Schumann accorde une grande importance aux lignes de basse. Celles-ci ne constituent pas seulement la base de l'harmonie, elles font aussi pleinement partie de l'écriture linéaire de la mélodie. On constate la prépondérance des graves même à des endroits où un rapport avec un autre matériau thématique n'est pas évident. De ce point de vue, l'exécution de larges écarts de la main gauche comme Schumann en demande pose de réelles difficultés. Au début de la deuxième sonate par exemple, les notes graves ne se contentent pas de faire pendant aux notes aiguës, elles représentent un élément essentiel de la construction du mouvement. Elles devraient être attaquées simultanément aux aigus (ou à la main droite) pour permettre de les moduler correctement en fonction de leur importance à l'aide de la pédale. Comme il est pratiquement impossible au pianiste de s'en sortir sans dissocier les accords, il pourrait exécuter un arpège rapide avec la note basse sur le temps fort. Cependant Schumann ayant l'habitude de mentionner les accords qu'il veut arpégés par un symbole d'arpège, il paraît préférable de jouer les notes graves de l'accord sur le temps fort et de donner les aigus tout de suite après.

Une autre difficulté réside dans les petites notes d'appoggiature dans les graves. Jamais gratuites chez Schumann, elles font intégralement partie de la composition et forment souvent la base de l'harmonie. En principe, depuis la deuxième partie du XVIIIe siècle, l'appoggiature précède de plus en plus souvent la note principale. L'interprète doit pourtant réfléchir dans quelle mesure elle doit ou peut être intégrée à l'accord principal. Il faut au moins mentionner un passage où il paraît indispensable de la lier à l'accord qui suit en une pédale harmonique, bien que la partition ne se déchiffre pas ainsi : dans l'Opus 105, aux mesures 206–209 du premier mouvement, la ligne cadencée de basse passe du *do* au *la* en passant les petites notes *ré* et *mi*. Sans la note fondamental *la*, le mouvement s'achèverait sur un accord sous la forme de 2e renversement.

À plusieurs endroits, Schumann indique sa volonté d'emploi de la pédale par les signes conventionnels, parfois seulement par l'expression plus générale *mit Pedal* [«avec pédale»]. Ces indications ont valeur d'exemple et fournissent de précieux renseignements, mais il ne faut pas oublier qu'à l'époque de Schumann, le piano ne possédait pas encore le volume sonore des instruments d'aujourd'hui, le son tenait moins longtemps et s'étouffait plus vite.

Bien entendu la pédale peut et doit être utilisée même si le compositeur ne le demande pas expressément. La règle à suivre est qu'il faut choisir son emploi en fonction du caractère de l'œuvre et en fonction de l'évolution harmonique et mélodique sans nuire à la ligne générale des voix.

En outre, employer la pédale ne signifie pas automatiquement l'enfoncer complètement ou la maintenir à fond, il faut au contraire faire preuve d'une grande sensibilité. Parfois il est bon d'en jouer avec une sorte de vibrato, notamment quand il s'agit de diminuer le son en decrescendo, comme le demandent les mesures 109 et 110 au premier mouvement de l'Opus 121 ainsi que leurs parallèles. On trouve un effet particulier de réverbération aux mesures 48–50 du mouvement central de l'Opus 105, où Schumann fait se superposer différentes harmonies à l'aide de la pédale. De tels fondus sonores – parfois déjà présents chez Beethoven – sont évidemment incontournables même s'ils requièrent une maîtrise très subtile de la pédale. À la mesure 71 du mouvement initial de l'Opus 121, un compromis de doigté est proposé pour le premier octave de basse, qui permet de changer de pédale sur la deuxième noire sans perdre la fondamentale. L'indication de Schumann *mit Ped.* [«avec pédale»] autorise cette solution. Le même doigté est à appliquer aux parallèles bien que cette indication de pédale ne figure pas à la mesure 239, un oubli peut-être. Dans l'Opus 121, premier mouvement, mesures 6sqq. et 20 – comme à d'autres endroits – le compositeur indique que la pédale doit être tenue au-delà des pauses indiquées.

Dans le troisième mouvement de l'Opus 121, Schumann utilise par moment la sourdine (*una corda*) comme un registre ou pour donner une nouvelle couleur sonore. Il emploie alors les expressions *mit Verschiebung* [«mettre la sourdine»] et *ohne Verschiebung* [«retirer la sourdine»].

L'interprète traitera avec le plus grand soin son jeu de pédale. S'il y prête une oreille attentive et critique, il parviendra bientôt à le varier en fonction de l'instrument et de la salle.

L'introduction du premier mouvement de l'Opus 121 renvoie par anagramme au dédicataire, le violoniste et ami du compositeur Ferdinand David. Schumann utilise pour les premières notes du thème initial les lettres du nom de famille en remplaçant le *v* par un *f* : *d″ - a′ - f″ - d″* (*ré″ - la′ - fa″ - ré″*). Ces mêmes notes – la deuxième à l'octave – forment le début du thème de *L'Art de la Fugue* de Jean-Sébastien Bach. Le caractère *ziemlich langsam* [«assez lent»] de l'introduction de Schumann et en particulier le rythme de la troisième mesure ne sont pas non plus sans évoquer la célèbre *Chaconne* en ré mineur de la Partita II pour violon seul BWV 1004 de Bach.

Peter Roggenkamp
(Traduction Sylvie Coquillat)

Violon

Le souhait de faire véritablement ressortir le son spécifique de Schumann est la principale raison pour les doigtés et la répartition de l'archet quelque peu orthodoxes.

Schumann avait une préférence marquée pour la position centrale sur le violon. Cette position produit les sons les plus «chauds», mais jamais de notes brillantes ou vraiment bruyantes. De même, l'écriture du piano, particulièrement dans l'opus 121, est plutôt dense et notre piano à queue moderne a un son plus volumineux que les instruments de l'époque de Schumann. Si l'on souhaite un dialogue équilibré entre le violon et le piano (moderne), il est recommandé d'utiliser le plus d'archet possible et aussi de bien répartir l'archet. La condition est une technique d'archet souple et la conscience d'une répartition originale de l'archet. Très souvent, dans la sonate op. 30 n° 1 de Beethoven déjà (premier mouvement), les liaisons sont à considérer comme des conseils de phrasé et non comme des prescriptions de technique d'archet. Ils sont impérativement à respecter comme signes de phrasé.

L'une des particularités de la technique d'archet est de grande importance pour le dernier mouvement de la sonate op. 105. Il y a une nette différence entre le *non legato* (tout le début) et le *spiccato*. Seuls les passages qui sont marqué en conséquence, donc  sont à jouer *spiccato*. Toutes les autres doubles croches doivent être jouées brièvement, si possible avec la moitié supérieure de l'archet, avec un léger *détaché* quelque peu éloigné de la corde. De cette manière, les vrais passages *spiccato* seront beaucoup plus marquants, voire «inquiétants» (dans le *pianissimo*), alors que les autres croches sonnent mieux accompagnées de celles du piano.

Christiane Edinger
(Traduction Sylvie Coquillat)

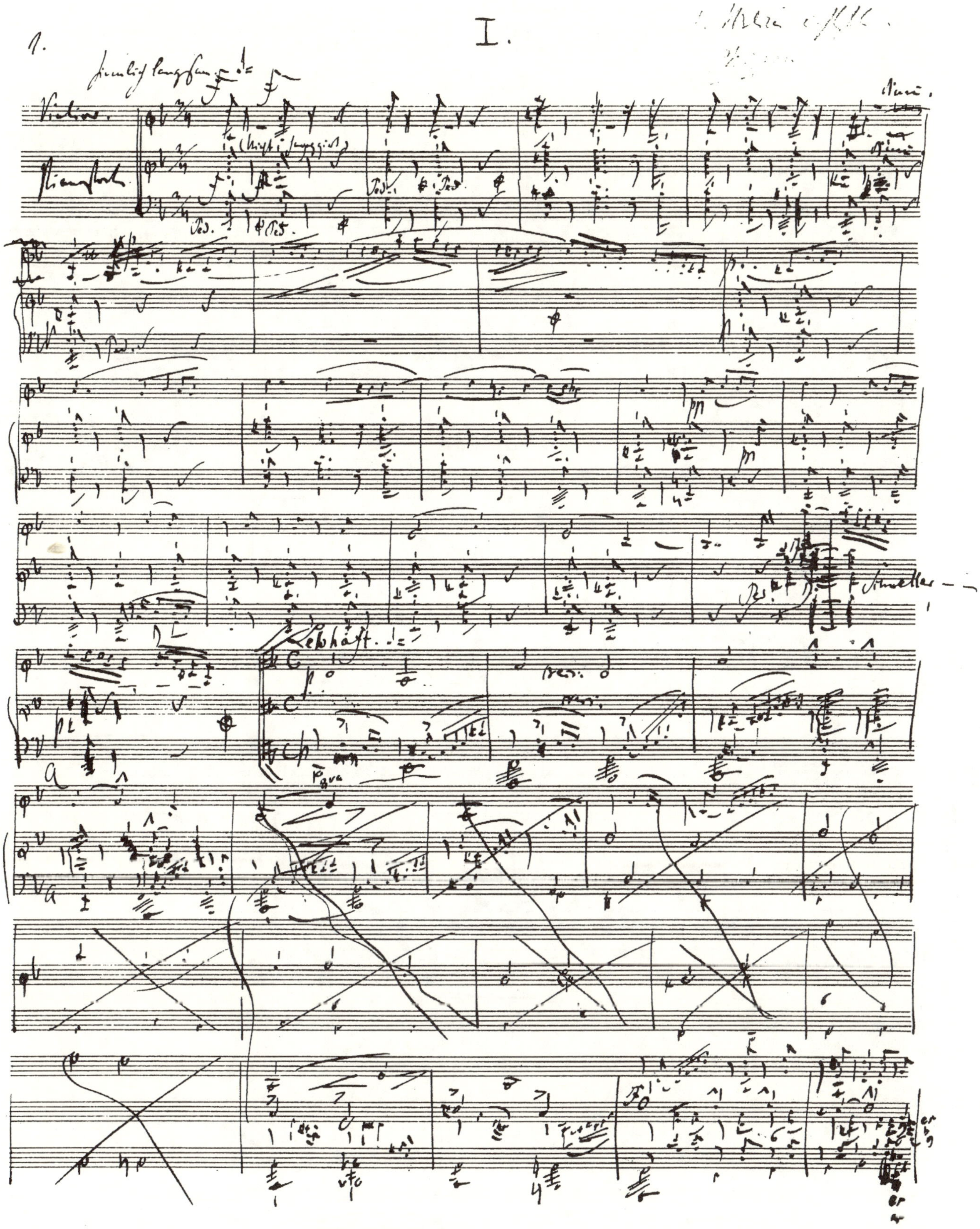

Robert Schumann, Sonate für Violine und Pianoforte in d-Moll (op. 121), 1. Satz
Arbeitsmanuskript Robert Schumanns, S. 1

Robert Schumann, Sonata for Violin and Piano in D minor (Op. 121), 1st movement
Working manuscript of Robert Schumann, p. 1

Robert Schumann, Sonate pour Violon et Piano en Ré mineur (op. 121), 1er mouvement
Manuscrit de travail de Robert Schumann, p. 1

(Heinrich-Heine-Institut, Düsseldorf, mit freundlicher Genehmigung)

SONATE

für Pianoforte und Violine

op. 105

Robert Schumann
(1810–1856)

I. Mit leidenschaftlichem Ausdruck ♩. = 68

© 2003 by Wiener Urtext Edition, Musikverlag, Ges.m.b.H. & Co. KG, Wien
Wiener Urtext Edition No. 50237

Das widerrechtliche Kopieren von Noten ist gesetzlich verboten und kann privat–und strafrechtlich verfolgt werden.
Unauthorised copying of music is forbidden by law, and may result in criminal or civil action.

10
p
cresc.
sf
cresc.
Ped.
13
sf
sf
16
sf
cresc.
cresc.
Ped.
20
f
sf
Ped.
Ped.
Ped.
Ped.

*) Siehe Einzelanmerkungen / See Detailed Notes / Voir Notes Détaillées

*) Siehe Einzelanmerkungen / See Detailed Notes / Voir Notes Détaillées

*) Siehe Einzelanmerkungen / See Detailed Notes / Voir Notes Détaillées

72
75
f
fp
sf
sfp
78
sfp
sfp
sfp
sfp

81
sfp
84
sf
86
p

89
91
93
cresc.
96

sf
f
Linke
p
cresc.
dim.
sf
Ped.

Etwas zurückhaltend
Etwas zurückhaltend
Im Tempo
Im Tempo
4te Saite
Ped.

123
cresc.
cresc.
126
130
cresc.
cresc.
134

*) Siehe Einzelanmerkungen / See Detailed Notes / Voir Notes Détaillées

*) Siehe Einzelanmerkungen / See Detailed Notes / Voir Notes Détaillées

166
cresc.
cresc.
Ped.
171
174
177
4te Saite

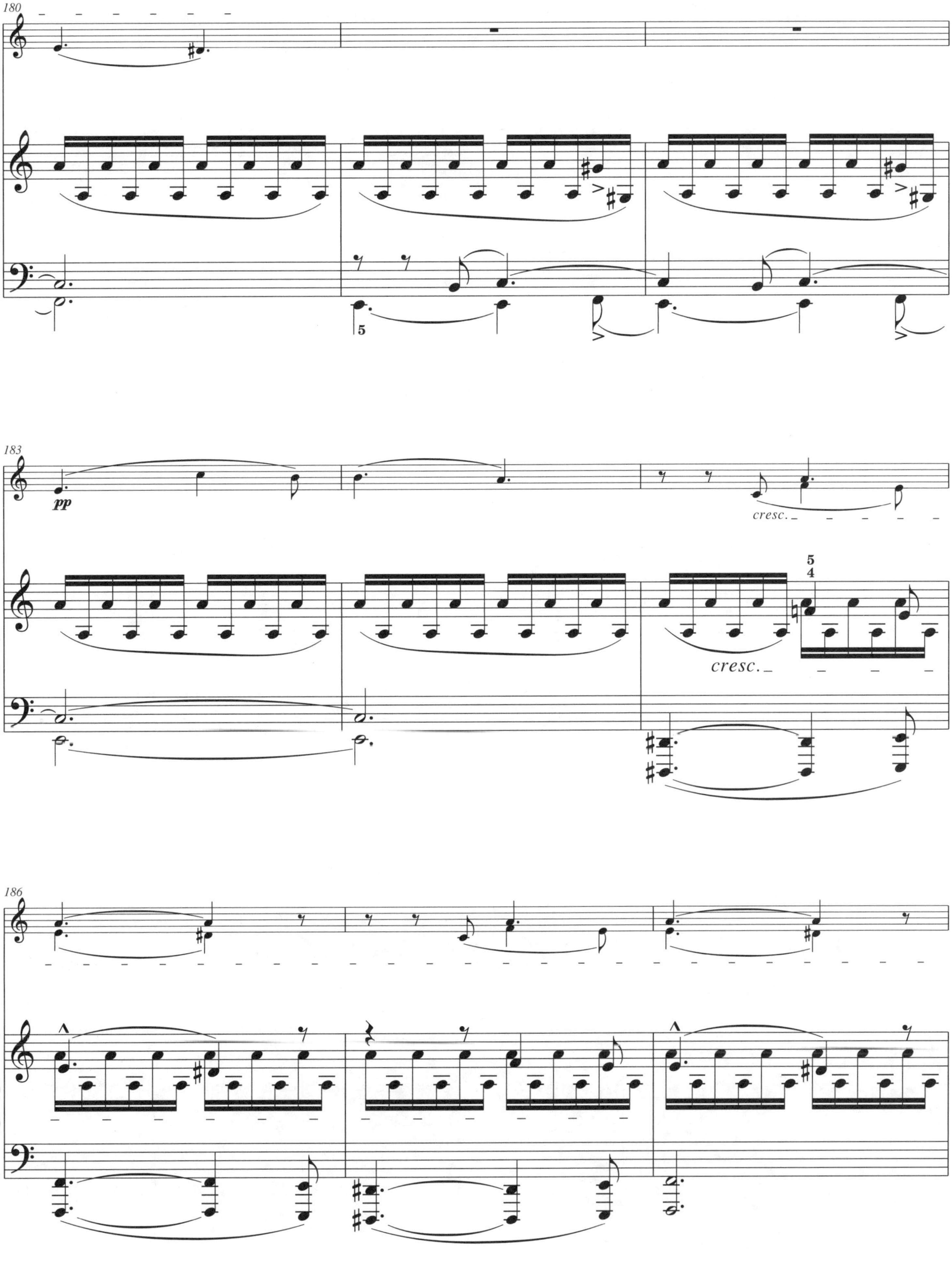
180
5
183
pp
cresc.
5
4
cresc.
186

189
192
195

198
cresc.
sf
cresc.
sf
201
Ped.
*
Ped.
*
205
sf
sf
sf
sf
1 2
sf
sf
sf
sf
Ped.
*
Ped.
*
Ped.
*
Ped.
*

Aus wendetechnischen Gründen bleibt diese Seite frei.
This page is left blank to avoid a difficult page turn.
Cette page est laissée en blanc pour éviter une tourne difficile.

II. Allegretto ♪ = 96

*) Siehe Einzelanmerkungen / See Detailed Notes / Voir Notes Détaillées

*) Siehe Einzelanmerkungen / See Detailed Notes / Voir Notes Détaillées

*) Siehe Einzelanmerkungen / See Detailed Notes / Voir Notes Détaillées

*) Dieser Bogen bedeutet, dass hier kein Arpeggio zu spielen ist. / Here the slur means no arpeggio. / Cette liaison veut dire pas d'arpège

III. Lebhaft ♩ = 94

*) Siehe Einzelanmerkungen / See Detailed Notes / Voir Notes Détaillées

32
37
42
cresc.
cresc.
47
cresc.
cresc.

52
57
1.
2.
cresc.
61
cresc.
66

4

88
92
97
102
tr
cresc.
cresc.

*) Siehe Einzelanmerkungen / See Detailed Notes / Voir Notes Détaillées

*) Siehe Einzelanmerkungen / See Detailed Notes /
Voir Notes Détaillées

*) Siehe Einzelanmerkungen / See Detailed Notes / Voir Notes Détaillées

158
tr
tr
cresc.
cresc.
163
cresc.
cresc.
168
4te Saite
172

*) Siehe Einzelanmerkungen / See Detailed Notes / Voir Notes Détaillées

193
198
203
208
cresc.
p cresc.
mit Ped.

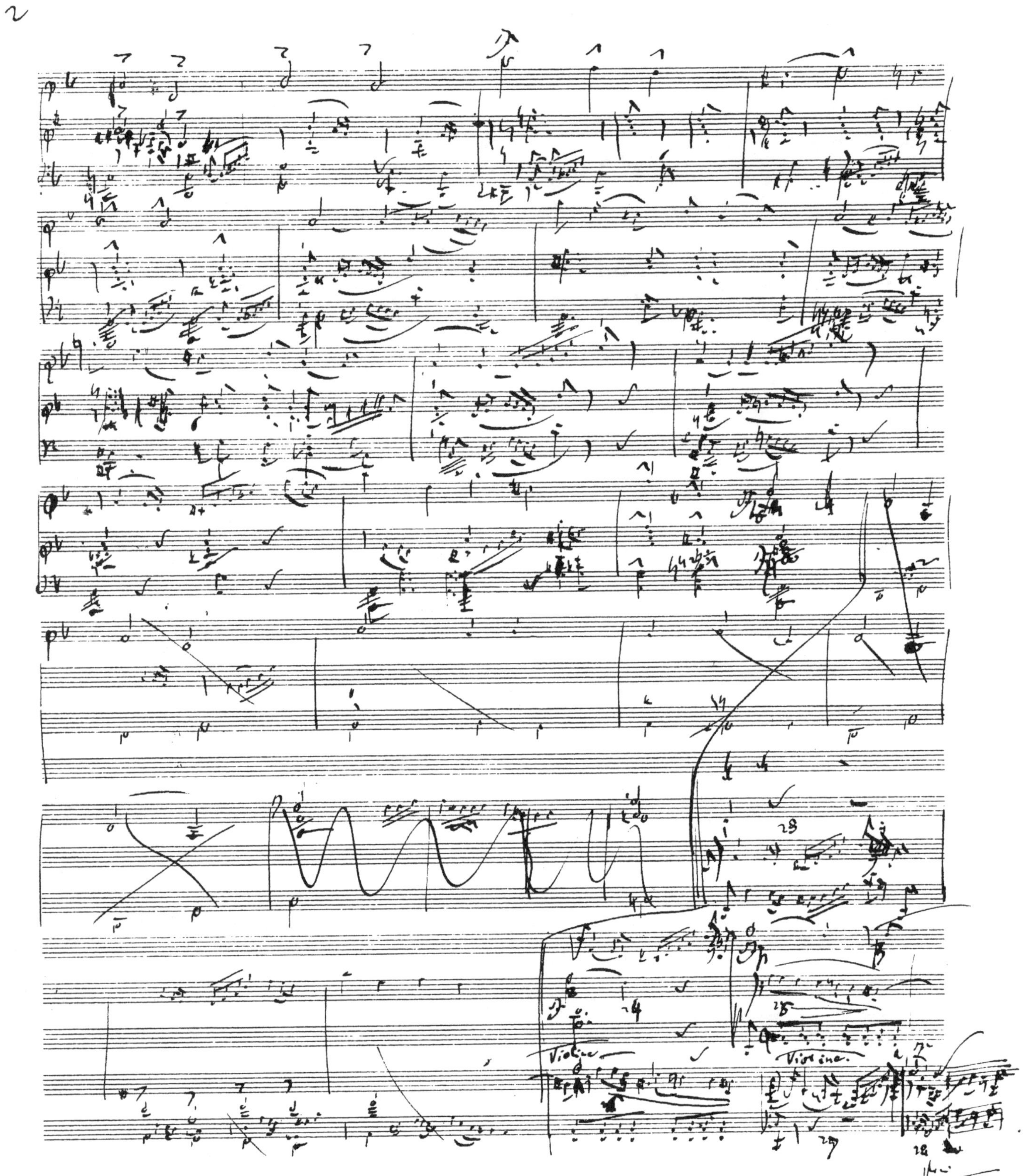

Robert Schumann, Sonate für Violine und Pianoforte in d-Moll (op. 121), 1. Satz
Arbeitsmanuskript Robert Schumanns, S. 2

Robert Schumann, Sonata for Violin and Piano in D minor (Op. 121), 1st movement
Working manuscript of Robert Schumann, p. 2

Robert Schumann, Sonate pour Violon et Piano en Ré mineur (op. 121), 1er mouvement
Manuscrit de travail de Robert Schumann, p. 2

(Heinrich-Heine-Institut, Düsseldorf, mit freundlicher Genehmigung)

Ferdinand David zugeeignet

2. GROSSE SONATE

für Violine und Pianoforte

op. 121

I. Ziemlich langsam ♩ = 46

*) Siehe Einzelanmerkungen / See Detailed Notes / Voir Notes Détaillées

mit Ped.
Etwas zurückhaltend
Etwas zurückhaltend
Im Tempo
Im Tempo

Ped.
mit Ped.

80
cresc.
cresc.
83
cresc.
cresc.
86
89
mit Ped.

92
ten.
ten.
ten.
ten.
1.
96b
2.
100
103

106
fp
fp
p
109
fp
p
Ped.
Ped.
112
fp
Ped.
114
sf
p
cresc.
sf
Ped.

117
Ped.
120
Ped.
123
Ped.
126
Linke
Ped.

129
sf
fp
sf
fp
p
Ped.
133
p
137
cresc.
sf
cresc.
f
sf
Ped.

Wiener Urtext Edition

UT 50237

Robert Schumann

Sonaten für Violine und Klavier
Sonatas for Violin and Piano
Sonates pour Violon et Piano

Band 1/Volume 1

Nach den Quellen herausgegeben von/Edited from the sources by/Edité d'après les sources par Ute Bär
Fingersätze und Hinweise zur Interpretation von/Fingering and Notes on Interpretation by/
Doigté et Notes sur l'Interprétation de
Christiane Edinger (Violine/violin/violon) und/and/et Peter Roggenkamp (Klavier/piano)

Violine

Wiener Urtext Edition, Schott/Universal Edition

Wiener Urtext Edition, Musikverlag Ges. m. b. H. & Co., K. G., Wien
Ein Gemeinschaftsunternehmen der Verlage Schott Music GmbH & Co. KG, Mainz, und Universal Edition, Wien

© 2003 by Wiener Urtext Edition, Musikverlag Ges. m. b. H. & Co., K. G., Wien · Printed in Germany
Vierte Auflage/Fourth Edition

ISMN 979-0-50057-257-2

SONATE

für Pianoforte und Violine
op. 105

Robert Schumann
(1810–1856)

I. **Mit leidenschaftlichem Ausdruck** ♩. = 68

© 2003 by Wiener Urtext Edition, Musikverlag, Ges.m.b.H. & Co. KG, Wien
Wiener Urtext Edition No. 50237

Das widerrechtliche Kopieren von Noten ist gesetzlich verboten und kann privat-und strafrechtlich verfolgt werden.
Unauthorised copying of music is forbidden by law, and may result in criminal or civil action.

*) Siehe Einzelanmerkungen / See Detailed Notes / Voir Notes Détaillées

*) Siehe Einzelanmerkungen / See Detailed Notes / Voir Notes Détaillées

cresc.
4te Saite
cresc.
cresc.

II. Allegretto ♪ = 96

*) Siehe Einzelanmerkungen / See Detailed Notes / Voir Notes Détaillées

*) Siehe Einzelanmerkungen / See Detailed Notes / Voir Notes Détaillées

III. Lebhaft ♩ = 94

*) Siehe Einzelanmerkungen / See Detailed Notes / Voir Notes Détaillées

cresc.
1.
2.
cresc.
D
tr
cresc.

*) Siehe Einzelanmerkungen / See Detailed Notes / Voir Notes Détaillées

tr
cresc.
4te Saite
cresc.
cresc.
cresc.

Ferdinand David zugeeignet

2. GROSSE SONATE

für Violine und Pianoforte

op. 121

I. Ziemlich langsam ♩ = 46

Etwas zurückhaltend
Im Tempo
D G
cresc.
cresc.
ten.
ten.
ten.
ten.

*) Siehe Einzelanmerkungen / See Detailed Notes / Voir Notes Détaillées

*) Siehe Einzelanmerkungen / See Detailed Notes / Voir Notes Détaillées

Etwas zurückhaltend
Im Tempo
cresc.

cresc.
ten.
ten.
G
Schneller

II. Sehr lebhaft ♩. = 112

dim.
cresc.
cresc.
cresc.
cresc.

153
159
164
169
immer schwächer und schwächer
173
178
185

190
cresc.
195
201
206
dim.
211
216
cresc.
221

III. Leise, einfach ♪ = 74

Etwas bewegter (Die 16tel Triolen wie im Scherzo die 8tel.)
am Steg bis *
cresc.
cresc.
Tempo wie vorher
D
D
cresc.
D Saite

Aus wendetechnischen Gründen bleibt diese Seite frei.
This page is left blank to avoid a difficult page turn.
Cette page est laissée en blanc pour éviter une tourne difficile.

IV. Bewegt ♩ = 110

dim.
cresc.

cresc.
cresc.

G
cresc.

103
106
109
112
115
118
120

dim.
cresc.
cresc.

cresc.
cresc.

WIENER URTEXT EDITION

Werke für Streicher und Bläser mit und ohne Klavier

	J. S. BACH
UT 50002	2 Sonaten für Violine und Basso continuo BWV 1021, 1023
UT 50018/19	6 Sonaten für Violine und Cembalo, 2 Bände BWV 1014–1019
UT 50255	Sonaten und Partiten für Violine solo BWV 1001 – 1006
UT 50133	Suiten für Violoncello solo BWV 1007–1012
UT 50260	Suite I für Violoncello solo G-Dur BWV 1007
	BEETHOVEN
UT 50017	Variationen über Volksweisen op. 105 / op. 107 für Klavier (und Flöte ad lib.)
UT 50247	Sonaten für Violoncello und Klavier (mit Violoncello-Fassung der Hornsonate op. 17)
	BRAHMS
UT 50015	Sonate für Klavier und Klarinette (oder Bratsche) f-Moll op. 120/1
UT 50016	Sonate für Klavier und Klarinette (oder Bratsche) Es-Dur op. 120/2
UT 50011	Sonate für Klavier und Violine G-Dur op. 78
UT 50012	Sonate für Klavier und Violine A-Dur op. 100
UT 50013	Sonate für Klavier und Violine d-Moll op. 108
UT 50039	Sonate für Klavier und Violoncello e-Moll op. 38
UT 50040	Sonate für Klavier und Violoncello F-Dur op. 99
	CORELLI
UT 50235/36	Violinsonaten op. 5, 2 Bände
	DEBUSSY
UT 50173	Syrinx „La Flûte de Pan“ für Flöte solo
	DVOŘÁK
UT 50162	Sonatine G-Dur op. 100 für Violine und Klavier
UT 50244	Werke für Violoncello und Klavier
	FRANCK
UT 50174	Sonate für Violine und Klavier
	HÄNDEL
UT 50264	Sonaten für Violine und Basso continuo
	MOZART
UT 50032–34	Sonaten für Klavier und Violine, 3 Bände
UT 50069	Variationen für Klavier und Violine
	REINECKE
UT 50242	Undine, Sonate für Flöte und Klavier op. 167
UT 50263	Undine, Sonate für Klarinette und Klavier op. 167
UT 50272	Sonaten für Violoncello und Klavier
	F. X. RICHTER
UT 50189	Sonaten für Flöte (Violine), Cembalo und Violoncello
	SCHUBERT
UT 50089	Sonate für Klavier und Violine D-Dur D 384 (op. 137/1)
UT 50004	Sonaten für Klavier und Violine
UT 50087	„Trockne Blumen“ für Klavier und Flöte D 802 (op. post. 160)
	SCHUMANN
UT 50237/38	Sonaten für Violine und Klavier, 2 Bände
	TELEMANN
UT 50187	12 Fantasien für Flöte solo
	VIVALDI
UT 50175	Sämtliche Sonaten für Violoncello und Basso continuo

Die Reihe wird fortgesetzt / This series will be continued

600S IX/2010

Printed in Germany · WEGA Mainz IX/11

141
145
148
151
Ped.

154
sf
pp
sf
p
Ped.
157
160
163
cresc.
cresc.

*) Siehe Einzelanmerkungen / See Detailed Notes / Voir Notes Détaillées

178
181
185
dim.
dim.
189
cresc.
cresc.

192
sf
Ped.
196
sf
Ped.
200
sf
Ped.
203
sf
Ped.

207
sf
sf
f
f
Ped.
*
210
sf
sf
f
f
sf
[Ped.]
[*]
213
sfp
sfp
f
p
f
Ped.
*
Ped.

216
219
222
Etwas zurückhaltend
Etwas zurückhaltend

225
Im Tempo
p
Im Tempo
pp
229
233
p
p
237

241
245
fp
fp
fp
fp
249
cresc.
cresc.

252
p
cresc.
p
cresc.
255
257
mit Ped.
260
sf
ten.
ten.
ff
ten.
ten.
sf
ff

265
cresc.
268
270
272

Schneller
Schneller

283
sfp
sfp
286
p
p
289
p
292
f
f
f
f

II. Sehr lebhaft ♩. = 112

24
30
36
41
dim.
cresc.

62
67
72

77
82
87
93

99
105
111
116
dim.
cresc.
dim.
cresc.

121
p
sf
fp
Ped.
*

136
cresc.
fp
cresc.
142
fp
p
cresc.
fp
fp
p
cresc.
Ped.
*
148
fp
fp
Ped.
*

153
158
p immer staccato
164
169
immer schwächer und schwächer
immer schwächer und schwächer

174
179
185
f
p
1
3
4

191
f
p
cresc.
3
196
f
202
ff
5
2
1
dim.

209
fp
fp
fp
1
fp
216
cresc.
cresc.
Ped.
*
221
f
f
f
sf
sf
f
Ped.
*
Ped.
*
Ped.
*
Ped.
*

III. Leise, einfach ♪ = 74

26
33
38
43

Etwas lebhafter
mf
Etwas lebhafter
mf
ohne Verschiebung

Etwas bewegter (Die 16tel Triolen wie im Scherzo die 8tel.)
Etwas bewegter (Die 16tel Triolen wie im Scherzo die 8tel.)
am Steg bis *
mit Verschiebung
ohne Verschiebung

cresc.
cresc.
Tempo wie vorher
Tempo wie vorher
mit Ped.

109
112
115
118

121
124
127
pp
p

130
cresc.
cresc.
133
p
p
pp
pp
136
D Saite

IV. Bewegt ♩ = 110

11
f
4
sf
sf
3
2
sf
13
sf
sf
ff
2
1
ff
16
sf
sf
19
1
2
2
1
sf
f
sf

nicht gebunden
nicht gebunden

30
32
34
36
dim.
dim.

38
p
4
5
p
3
2
40
4
2
42
2
3
1
4
44
cresc.
1
cresc.
3
5

46
48
50
cresc.
cresc.
52
f
f
sf

54
sf
f
56
sf
sf
58
p
p
62

65
cresc.
cresc.
68
p
p
sf
70
p
p
sf
72

85
88
91
94
Ped.
p

*) Siehe Einzelanmerkungen / See Detailed Notes /
Voir Notes Détaillées

105
108
110
112

114
116
119
122
nicht gebunden

124
p
nicht gebunden
126
[1]
sfp
sfp
128
[1]
p
130
sf

132
134
136
dim.
dim.
138

140
142
144
cresc.
cresc.
146

148
150
cresc.
cresc.
152
155

158
160
cresc.
cresc.
162
164
p
cresc.
p
cresc.

166
169
171
174
f
p
p

KRITISCHE ANMERKUNGEN

Abkürzungen

a. rev.	vor Revision
Bg(n).	Bogen (Bögen)
gem.	gemäß
Hbg(n).	Haltebogen (-bögen)
korr.	korrigiert
l.N.	letzte Note
NA	vorliegende Neuausgabe
OS	Oberstimme
o.S.	oberes System
Pf	Pianoforte (beide Systeme)
Pfo	Pianoforte, oberes System
Pfu	Pianoforte, unteres System
PN	Plattennummer
p. rev .	nach Revision
Pst(n).	Parallelstelle(n)
Pt.	Paralleltakt(e)
stacc.-Pkt(e).	*staccato*-Punkt(e)
stacc.-Str.	*staccato*-Strich(e)
Vl	Violine
US	Unterstimme
u.S.	unteres System
vs.	versehentlich
zw.	zwischen
→	angeglichen an

1. Violinsonate op. 105

Quellen

AM Autographes Arbeitsmanuskript (Düsseldorf, 12.–16. September 1851). Vollständige Niederschrift der 3 Sätze einschließlich zahlreicher verworfener Textteile, Korrekturen und Anweisungen für den Kopisten von Robert Schumann.
Paris, Bibliothèque Nationale, Département de la Musique, Ms. 331.

OP, OV Originalausgabe: Klavierpartitur (**OP**) und separate Violinstimme (**OV**). Erschienen im Verlag Friedrich Hofmeister, Leipzig, Januar 1852. PN: 4508.
Sonate / (in A moll) / für / Pianoforte und Violine / componirt von / ROBERT SCHUMANN / Op. 105. Pr. 2 Thlr. / Eigenthum der Verleger / Eingetragen ins Vereins Archiv. / LEIPZIG, BEI FRIEDRICH HOFMEISTER. / Paris bei S. Richault. ... London bei Ewer & C°
Zwickau, Robert-Schumann-Haus; Archiv-Nr.: 94.41$^{a/b}$ – D1.

PR,VR Klavierpartitur und separate Violinstimme der Ausgabe von Simon Richault. Erschienen vermutlich 1853 in Paris. PN: 12.602. R.
Paris, Bibliothèque Nationale, Département de la Musique, Ms. VM 15 5345.

Quellenbewertung und Edition

Die Werkgenese ist in den Quellen nur lückenhaft dokumentiert. Überliefert sind lediglich das Arbeitsmanuskript (**AM**), die autorisierte Originalausgabe (**OP, OV**) sowie Klavierpartitur und Solostimme des bei Simon Richault in Paris erschienenen Druckes (**PR, VR**). Als Stichvorlagen dienende Abschriften (vgl. Schumanns Kopieranweisungen in **AM**) sowie Korrekturfahnen fehlen. In der Druckphase nahm Schumann, wie Unterschiede zwischen **AM**, **OP** und **OV** zeigen, Korrekturen vor. In der verschollenen Abschrift der separaten Solostimme und in der Violinstimme der Partiturabschrift müssen Änderungen erfolgt sein, die jedoch nicht wechselseitig abgeglichen worden sind. Dies belegen Unterschiede zwischen **OV** und der Solopartie in **OP**. Es ist anzunehmen, dass **OV** nach der Stimmenabschrift mit den hierin vorgenommenen, nicht in die Abschrift der Klavierpartitur übertragenen Korrekturen gestochen wurde. Für die Violinstimme in **OP** bildete dagegen die Partiturabschrift die Grundlage.

Die Originalausgabe bildet somit als Fassung letzter Hand die Hauptquelle. In der vorliegenden Ausgabe folgt die Klavierstimme **OP**, die Violinstimme bei Unterschieden zwischen **OP** und **OV** der jeweils differenzierteren Variante. Bei Varianten bzw. widersprüchlichen Lesarten wurde **AM** konsultiert, um die korrekte Lesart zu ermitteln. An Stellen, an denen die Edition **AM** folgt, sind die Abweichungen von **OP** bzw. **OV** in den Einzelanmerkungen angegeben. Ließen sich die Divergenzen zwischen **OP** und **OV** nicht durch einen Vergleich mit **AM** klären, wurde der differenzierteren Lesart der Vorzug gegeben bzw. im Vergleich zu Parallelstellen die jeweils plausibelste Version gewählt. Dabei wird in den Einzelanmerkungen die Bezugsquelle (**OP** oder **OV**) nicht nochmals explizit benannt. Unterschiedliche Lesarten an von Schumann eindeutig als Wiederholungen ausgewiesenen Parallelstellen sind in der Regel einander angeglichen worden, wobei jeweils der differenzierteren Variante der Vorzug gegeben wurde. In begründeten Einzelfällen behält die Edition jedoch die Unterschiede in Dynamik bzw. Artikulation bei. Bei unterschiedlicher Angabe von *staccato*-Punkt bzw. *staccato*-Strich ist in der vorliegenden Ausgabe in Zweifelsfällen ein *staccato*-Strich notiert worden, da Schumann in **AM** und der autorisierten Originalausgabe, vor allem im 3. Satz, wie die Parallelstellen zeigen, offenbar nicht eindeutig zwischen Punkt und Strich unterschied, T. 198 in **OV** aber *staccato*-Striche aus *staccato*-Punkten korrigiert hat. In der Schreibweise von aufeinander folgenden Legato- und Haltebögen orientiert sich die vorliegende Ausgabe im Unterschied zur Neuen Schumann-Gesamtausgabe an der Notationspraxis der Originalausgabe.

Ergänzungen des Herausgebers im Notentext sind durch eckige Klammern kenntlich gemacht. Vom Herausgeber hinzugefügte Warnungsakzidentien sind nicht durch Klammern gekennzeichnet.

Die Einzelanmerkungen folgen dem Schema: Takt – System / Stimme – Zeichen im Takt (Note oder Pause) bzw. Zählzeit – Bemerkung.

Einzelanmerkungen

1. Satz

Vl: $<$ bzw. $>$ gem. **OV**: T. 4, 15, 84–85, 110–111, 112, 118, 205

2	Vl	**OP, OV**: *cresc.* fehlt; NA → Pf, **AM**
10	Pf	**OP**: $<$ ab Zz. 2+

17	Pf	Zz. 1–6	**OP, AM:**  ; in NA korr. gem. **OP** Pt. 131
19–22	Vl		**OP:** *cresc.* ab T. 19, Zz. 1, Fortführungsstriche fehlen
	Pf		**AM:** Fortführungsstriche zu *cresc.* fehlen; in **OP** bis T. 21 Ende; NA → Vl
29	Pf		**AM:** < fehlt; **OP:** < ab Zz. 5; NA → Pt. 143
36, 150	Pfo OS	Zz. 4	**AM:** ♪(*h'* bzw. *g'*) und Hbg. fehlen; **OP:** Zz. 3–4 *h'* bzw. *g'* als ♩; NA → Vl sowie T. 40 bzw. 154
47–49	Vl		> in den Quellen unterschiedlich; NA: Beginn gem. **OP**, Ende gem. **OV**
	Pf		<: **AM, OP:** T. 47, Zz. 4 – T. 47 Ende, >: **AM:** T. 48, Zz. 3–6; **OP:** T. 48 Zz. 1–5; NA → Vl
51–52	Pfo OS	Zz. 4–6	**OP:** Bgn. fehlen
55	Pf		**OP:** ***f*** erst T. 56, 1
57	Vl	Zz. 6	**OP:** ♯ zu *cis''* fehlt
59–60	Pfu		in **AM** nicht ausgeschrieben; **OP:** Bgn. T. 59, Zz. 4 – T. 60, Zz. 3 geteilt (Akkoladenwechsel); in NA korr. nach o.S., T. 61–62, 173–174
63–64	Vl		**OP:** Oktavierung von **AM** nicht ausgeführt
66	Vl	2	**AM, OP, OV:** ♫; NA → T. 2
		Zz. 4–6	**OP, OV:** mit Bgn.; NA gem. **AM** T. 2
68	Vl		> gem. **AM; OP:** > 2–3;
69	Pfo OS	Zz. 3–4	**AM, OP:** *cis''* als ♩; NA → T. 70
75	Pfo	Zz. 4–6	**OP:** OS und US vertauscht
76	Pfo	Zz. 5	**OP:** *stacc.*-Pkt. fehlt
78	Pfo	Zz. 4	**OP:** ♭ zu *b'* vs. im 3. Zwischenraum
79	Pfu	Zz. 3	**OP:** ♮ zu *f* vs. vor *g*
80	Pfu	Zz. 4	**OP:** ♯ zu *cis* fehlt, erst zu Zz. 6 vorhanden
85	Vl		**AM:** > fehlt; **OP, OV:** unterschiedlich; NA → Pf
	Pfu		**OP:** ***f*** statt ***sf***; NA → **AM** T. 87
86–87	Pf		**OP:** < > unter u.S.; NA → T. 84–85
94	Vl		**OP, AM:** *cresc.* zw. *e'* und *g'*
105	Pfu US	Zz. 5	**OP:** 𝅀 statt 𝄾
106	Vl		**OP:** *cresc.* erst nach Zz. 1
108	Pfo	1	**OP:** ♩ statt ♪
110, 114	Pf		**OP:** ✻ nach Zz. 5; NA → T. 111–112
113–115	Vl		Lbg. gem. **OV**
124	Pf		**OP:** < ab Zz. 1+; NA → **AM** Pt. 10
133–136	Vl		**OP:** *cresc.* ab T. 133, Zz. 4, Fortführungsstriche bis T. 133 Ende; NA → **OV** Pt. 19–22
	Pf		**OP:** Fortführungsstriche zu *cresc.* bis T. 133 Ende; NA → Pt. 19–22
141–142	Pfo	Zz. 4–3	**OP:** Achtelhälse für US fehlen
	Pfu		**OP:** Bg. T. 141, US 2 – T. 142, US 3; NA → Pt. 27–28
145	Pfo	Zz. 4–6	**OP:** OS und US vertauscht, Bg. zu Sechzehnteln (= OS); NA korr. nach Pt. 31 und **AM**
145–146	Pf		**AM, OP:** ***sf*** über o.S.; NA → T. 32–33, T. 147
158	Pfo	Zz. 4–6	**OP:**  ; NA → **AM**, Pt. 44
161–163	Vl		**OP, OV:** < unterschiedlich; NA gem. Wiederholungsvorlage in **AM**
	Vl		> in den Quellen unterschiedlich; NA → Pt. 48–49
	Pf		**AM:** < > fehlt in der Wiederholungsvorlage; **OP:** < T. 161, Zz. 4–6, > T. 162, Zz. 1–6; NA → Vl
163	Vl		**OP:** ***p*** fehlt
165–166	Pfo OS	Zz. 4–6	**OP:** Bgn. fehlen
168	Pf		**AM:** ✻ fehlt; **OP:** ✻ zw. Zz. 4 und 5; NA → Pt. 54
	Pfo		**OP:** Bg. Zz. 1–6; NA → Pt. 54
169	Pf		**OP:** ***f*** erst T. 170
186, 188	Pfo	Zz. 1–3	**AM:** Bgn. fehlen; **OP:** Bgn. zu US; NA → Vl
189–190	Vl		Fingersätze gem. **OV**
198	Pf		**AM:** *cresc.* fehlt; **OP:** zw. Zz. 3 und 4; NA → Vl

2. Satz

2	Pf		**OP:** *rit.* zw. Zz. 1 und 2; NA gem. **AM**, Vl
5	Pfo	2	**OP:** 𝄾 statt 𝅀
5–6	Pfu		**AM:** Bg. über Taktende hinaus; **OP:** Bg. T. 5, 3–5; NA → Pfo
8, 33	Vl	5	**AM, OP:** mit *stacc.*-Pkt.; NA → T. 9–10, **OV**
9	Vl	10	**OP:** mit *stacc.*-Pkt.; NA → Pt. 34, **OV**
10, 35	Vl	1	**OV:** ***sfp*** statt >
13–14	Vl		**OP, OV:** Hbg. *h–h* fehlt
14			*rit.* in allen Quellen unterschiedlich; NA → Pt. 2, 7, 39
27	Vl		**AM:** < 2–6; **OP, OV:** < fehlt; NA → Pt. 2
28	Vl		**AM:** > T. 27. l.N. – T. 28, 1; **OP, OV:** > fehlt; NA → Pt. 3
30–31, 61–62	Pfu		**OP:** Bg. T. 30, 3–5; NA → Pfo
35	Vl	3–4	**OP:** *stacc.*-Pkte. fehlen
38–39	Vl		**OP, OV:** Hbg. *h–h* fehlt
45	Vl	1	**AM, OV:** ***f*** fehlt
47–48	Vl		**AM:** Bg. fehlt; **OP:** 2 Bgn.: 1. Bg. T. 47, 1–4, 2. Bg. T. 48, 1–3; NA gem. **OV**
56	Vl		**AM:** ***p*** statt *dim.*; **OP, OV:** *dimin.* zw. Zz. 1 und 2; NA → Pf
58	Pfo	1	**OP:** vs. ♪ statt 𝅘𝅥𝅯

63	Vl		< 2–6 gem. **OV**
64	Vl	3–4	*stacc.*-Pkte. gem. **OV**
65	Vl	6–8	Bg. gem. **OV**
66	Pfo	3	**OP**: vs. ♯ vor *es'*, ♭ vor *fis'*
67	Pf		**AM**: *dim.* fehlt; **OP**: *dimin.* zw. Zz. 1 und 2; NA → Vl
77–78	Vl		Bg. bis T. 78, 1 gem. **OV**

3. Satz

Vl: < / > gem. **OV**: T. 31–32, 36, 54–55, 87–88, 90–91, 108, 157
Vl: *staccati* gem. **OV**: T. 8, 13, 58a/b, 129, 180, 189, 191 u. 201: jeweils 1. Note; T. 204, l.N.

2	Pf		**OP**: < bis T. 3, 1; NA gem. Pt. 18, 118, 134, **AM**
13	Vl	1, 4	**OP**: *stacc.*-Striche aus *stacc.*-Punkten korr. (Pt. 129 aber *stacc.*-Punkte); NA gem. **OV**
18	Vl		**OP**: < bis T. 19, 2; **OV**: > bis T. 18, l.N.; NA → Pt. 2
27–28	Pf		**AM**: Ped., * fehlen; **OP**: * nach T. 27, l.N.; NA → Pt. 143f.
29	Vl	2	***p*** gem. **OV**
31–32	Pfu		**OP**: T. 32: Bg.-Ende fehlt; **AM**: Bg. nur T. 32
40	Vl	5	**OP**: zusätzlicher *stacc.*-Pkt.; NA gem. **OV**
46	Pfo		**OP**: Bg. fehlt
55–56	Pfo		**AM**, **OP**: Bg. nur bis T. 54, l.N.
	Pfu		**OP**: Bg. fehlt
61	Vl		*cresc.* ab Zz. 1 gem. **OV**
65, 66	Vl	1, 4	∧ gem. **OV**, vgl. auch T. 69, 71, 73–74
84–86	Vl		**OP**: < T. 84, Zz. 2 – T. 85, 1 (3. Triolenachtel); **OV**: 1. < T. 84, Zz. 2 – T. 85, Zz. 1 (2. Triolenachtel), 2. < T. 86, Zz. 1 – T. 87, Zz. 1 (Akkoladenwechsel); NA: korr. < T. 84, Zz. 2 – T. 87, Zz. 1
	Pf		**OP**: 1. < T. 84, Zz. 2 – T. 85, l.N., 2. < T. 86, Zz. 2 – Taktende; NA → Vl
107	Vl		**OP**: *cresc.* 2. statt 1. Note
109	Vl	4	**OP**: *stacc.*-Strich und *stacc.*-Punkt übereinander gestochen, ohne die ursprüngliche Lesart zu tilgen, **OV**: *stacc.*-Strich statt *stacc.*-Punkt; NA gem. Pstn. T. 112–114, **AM**
111	Vl	4	**OP**: ***p*** statt ***pp***; NA gem. **OV**
117	Vl	4	**OP**: *stacc.*-Punkt und *stacc.*-Strich übereinander gestochen, ohne ursprüngliche Lesart zu tilgen; NA gem. **OV**
118–119	Vl		< in den Quellen unterschiedlich; NA: Beginn gem. **OV**, Ende gem. **OP**
121–122	Pf		**OP**: < erst ab T. 122 (= T. 6 der Wiederholungsvorlage von **AM** Akkoladen- bzw. Seitenwechsel); NA → Pt. 5–6
124	Vl	1	*stacc.*-Pkt. gem. **OP** Pt. 8
129	Pfu	1	**OP**: ∧ zu o.S. 1; NA → Pt. 13, **AM**
137	Vl	1	∧ gem. **AM** Pt. 21
143	Pfo	1	**OP**: zusätzlicher ∧
	Pfu	1	**OP**: *stacc.*-Pkt. statt *stacc.*-Str.
144	Pf		**AM**: * fehlt; **OP**: * zw. 3. und 4. ♪
147	Vl	1	***f*** gem. **OV**
150–151	Pfo		**OP**: ursprünglich *stacc.*-Punkte, *stacc.*-Striche darüber gestochen, ohne die ursprüngliche Lesart zu tilgen
	Pfu		**OP**: *stacc.*-Pkte. statt *stacc.*-Str.; NA → o.S.
162	Vl		**OP**, **OV**: *cresc.* nach Zz. 1; NA → Pt. 46, **AM**
168	Vl		**OV**: *4te Saite* erst T. 169, 1; NA → **OP**, 1. Satz, T. 1
172–173	Vl		**OP**, **OV**: < > fehlt
177	Vl	5	Fingersatz gem. **OV**
185	Pf		**OP**: Ped. bereits T. 184, Zz. 2+
186–187	Pf		**OP**: * T. 186–187 Zz. 2+; NA: T. 185–187 Pedalnotation vereinheitlicht
188	Vl	1	**OP**: ∧ ; **OV**: *stacc.*-Str.; NA → T. 189–192
192	Vl	1	***f*** gem. **OV**
202–203	Vl		**OP**: *stacc.*-Pkte. statt *stacc.*-Str.; NA gem. **OV**
205	Pfo	1	**OP**: *stacc.*-Pkt. fehlt
209	Pfo	1	**OP**: *a''* fehlt

2. Violinsonate op. 121

Quellen

SK Skizzen zum 1. Satz der Klavierpartitur (Düsseldorf, spätestens 26. Oktober 1851). Zwickau, Robert-Schumann-Haus, Archiv-Nr.: 10398 – A1.

AM Arbeitsmanuskript, in zwei getrennten Teilen überliefert.
Teil 1: vollständige Niederschrift der Sätze I–IV (Düsseldorf, 26. Oktober – 4. November 1851).
Nachträglich hinzugefügter Bogen mit Neufassung der Klavierbegleitung zum 4. Satz, T. 35–51 (= **AMR**).
Teil 2: verworfene Fassung der Takte 62–94 des 4. Satzes (Düsseldorf, 29. Oktober – 2. November 1851).
Düsseldorf, Heinrich-Heine-Institut, Akzessions-Nr.: 74.118 und 97.5046 G.

SP, RV Stichvorlage zur Originalausgabe der Klavierpartitur (**SP**) und Reinschrift der separaten Violinstimme (**RV**), (Düsseldorf, 4. – 15. November 1851). Kopist: Peter Fuchs, Vorlage: **AM**.
SP: Niederschrift des 1.–3. Satzes (bis T. 129) und T. 11–185 des 4. Satzes. Ein Einzelblatt mit T. 130–140 des 3. und T. 1–10 des 4. Satzes verschollen.
Lücken im Notentext aufgrund entsprechender Anweisungen Robert Schumanns und Unleserlichkeit stark korrigierter Stellen in **AM** (z.B. Violinstimme, 1. Satz, T. 1–6, von R. Schumann in **AM** gestrichen, später ergänzt durch Clara Schumann).

	Zwei Revisionen: Komplettierung der von Fuchs belassenen Textlücken durch R. Schumann, Korrektur von Schreibfehlern, Zusatz von Bögen, dynamischen und artikulatorischen Zeichen, in der 2. Revision auch Konzeptionsänderungen. Danach noch wiederholte Korrekturen durch R. und Cl. Schumann (u. a. Neufassung von T. 35–51 und 134–150 im 4. Satz) auf Grundlage der Neufassung des Klavierparts in **AM**. Zahlreiche Ergänzungen Cl. Schumanns, besonders an den von R. Schumann in **AM** nicht ausgeschriebenen Parallelstellen. Eintragungen von fremder Hand. Abschließende Durchsicht (*Revidirt / d. 13.10.52*) durch R. Schumann. Zahlreiche Stechereintragungen. **RV**: Aus **SP** ausgezogene Reinschrift, aber nicht völlig identisch mit Violinstimme in **SP**. Veränderungen durch R. Schumann bei der Durchsicht. Ferner Ergänzungen und Korrekturen von Cl. Schumann, Wilhelm Joseph von Wasielewski (erster Interpret der Solopartie) sowie möglicherweise von Ferdinand David, der auch aus **RV** spielte. Außerdem Fingersätze, vermutlich von Wasielewski (vor allem im 4. Satz), Warnungsakzidentien und enharmonische Notierung (mit ♯) von T. 97 des 4. Satzes zur Leseerleichterung. Änderungen bzw. Ergänzungen in **SP** und **RV** im Zuge der Probeaufführungen, nicht wechselseitig abgeglichen. Carpentras, Bibliothèque Inguimbertine, MS 1071.
OP, OV	Originalausgabe: Klavierpartitur (**OP**) und separate Violinstimme (**OV**). Erschienen im September 1853 bei Breitkopf & Härtel in Leipzig. PN: 8761. *2te. / GROSSE SONATE / FÜR / Violine und Pianoforte / FERDINAND DAVID / zugeeignet / VON / Robert Schumann. / Op. 121. / Eigenthum der Verleger. / Leipzig, bei Breitkopf & Härtel. / Pr. 2 Thlr. 15 Ngr. / Eingetragen in das Vereinsarchiv. / 8761. / Entd. Sta. Hall.* Düsseldorf, Robert-Schumann-Forschungsstelle, Sammlung Fink, Inv.-Nr.: 911

Quellenbewertung und Edition

In der reichen Quellenüberlieferung ist die Werkgenese nahezu lückenlos dokumentiert. Dabei enthalten die Abschriften **SP** und **RV** verschiedene Revisionen, die nicht gegenseitig abgeglichen wurden. **SP** diente aber zweifelsfrei als Stichvorlage für die Originalausgabe (**OP** und **OV**). **RV** war zwar nicht Stichvorlage für **OV**, wirkte auf die Textgestaltung der Originalausgabe aber noch mittelbar ein, denn die Violinstimme in **OP** und **OV** enthält die in **RV** eingetragenen Ergänzungen und Korrekturen. Der Abgleich hinsichtlich der zwischen den Abschriften bestehenden Varianten muss in der Phase der von Schumann überwachten Drucklegung vorgenommen worden sein. Der konkrete Stichverlauf der Violinstimme ist aber nicht mehr nachvollziehbar, da die Korrekturfahnen verschollen sind. Auch sind in den von Schumann in **AM** ausgewiesenen Wiederholungspassagen in **OP** und **OV** zahlreiche Angleichungen vorhanden, die in den beiden Abschriften fehlen. Schumann hat demnach in der Druckphase noch in den Notentext eingegriffen.

Für die vorliegende Ausgabe bildet demzufolge die Originalausgabe (**OP** und **OV**) die Hauptquelle. Obwohl es sich hierbei um die autorisierte Fassung letzter Hand handelt, bedarf die kritische Revision des Notentextes des Rückbezugs auf frühere Textstadien, um widersprüchliche Lesarten in die korrekte Lesart zu überführen. In diesen Fällen wird vor allem die Stichvorlage **SP** als Referenzquelle für die Ausgabe herangezogen. Die Einbeziehung von **AM** erfolgt dann, wenn auch **SP** nicht hinreicht, die korrekte Lesart zu bestimmen. Wo dies nicht möglich ist, wird im Vergleich zu Parallelstellen die jeweils plausibelste Version gewählt. Unterschiedliche Varianten in den von Schumann eindeutig als Reprisen ausgewiesenen Parallelstellen sind in der Regel angeglichen worden, wobei jeweils der differenzierteren Variante der Vorzug gegeben wurde.

In der Schreibweise von aufeinander folgenden Legato- und Haltebögen orientiert sich die vorliegende Ausgabe im Unterschied zur Neuen Schumann-Gesamtausgabe an der Notationspraxis der Originalausgabe.

Ergänzungen des Herausgebers im Notentext sind wiederum durch eckige Klammern gekennzeichnet. Vom Herausgeber hinzugefügte Warnungsakzidentien sind nicht durch Klammern gekennzeichnet.

Die folgenden Einzelanmerkungen dokumentieren die Unterschiede zwischen der Hauptquelle und der vorliegenden Ausgabe. Ungenauigkeiten der Hauptquelle in Artikulation, Dynamik oder Pedalangaben, die aus Platzgründen erfolgten, werden in der Ausgabe stillschweigend reguliert. So ist z.B. in **OP** im 1. Satz, T. 6, 31, 33, 114, 119–120, 129–130, 139, 145, 149–150, 199 *Ped.* jeweils vor, im 3. Satz, T. 91 nach der Note des Pedalbeginns, *dim.* in Vl und Pf im 1. Satz, T. 17 nach dem beabsichtigten Beginn gestochen worden. Bei abweichender Notierung in der Violinstimme von **OP** und **OV** wird die ungültige Variante erwähnt, die gültige Bezugsquelle jedoch nicht nochmals benannt. Die Einzelanmerkungen folgen dem Schema: Takt – System / Stimme – Zeichen im Takt (Note oder Pause) bzw. Zählzeit – Bemerkung.

Einzelanmerkungen

1. Satz

7–8	Vl		< > in allen Quellen uneinheitlich; NA gem. **AM**
8	Pf		* auf Zz. 2 gem. **SP**
24	Pfu	1	*stacc.*-Str. gem. Pt. 192
		Zz. 4+	*arpeggio*-Zeichen gem. Pt. 192
25	Vl		**OP**:  ; **OV**: < > zu *e′*; NA gem. **RV**
27	Pf		**AM**: *Ped.* fehlt
31, 199	Pfu OS	Zz. 1	𝄾 gem. **OP**
45–46	Pf		> in den Quellen uneinheitlich, ebenso in Pt. 109–110, 113–114, 119–120, 125–126, 213–214; in NA Gabelende stets wie T. 45–46 reguliert
57–58	Vl		< > gem. **SP**, **RV**, **OV**
60	Vl		**OV**: < > mittig zw. Zz. 1 und 2

72	Vl		< gem. **SP**
128	Pf	1	**OP**: ***sf*** fehlt
169	Vl	2	**AM**: *as*; **SP**, **RV**: vs. *b*; Fehler in **OP**, **OV** übernommen
213	Pf		**SP**, **OP**: ***p*** erst Zz. 1+; NA → Pt. 45, **AM**
224	Vl		**OP**: 1. Bg. 2–6 statt 2–7
226	Vl		**OV**: > Zz. 1–3
229–230	Vl		< > gem. **OV** (gegenüber Pt. 61 veränderte Notierung, möglicherweise aber kein Interpretationsunterschied beabsichtigt)
238–239	Pf		**AM**: keine Pedalangaben in der Wiederholungsvorlage für die nicht ausgeschriebenen T. 226–250; **SP**, **OP**: unterschiedliche Pedalangaben; NA: Pedalnotation gem. **OP** (gegenüber Pt. 70–71 verändert, möglicherweise aber kein Interpretationsunterschied beabsichtigt)
240	Pf		**OP**: < bereits ab Zz. 2+; NA gem. Pt. 72, **SP**
247	Vl		**OP**: Bg. 4–8 statt 3–8
249	Vl, Pf		**OP**: *cresc.* Zz. 1+; NA → Pt. 81, **OV**, **SP**
285–286	Pfu		**OP**: Hbgn. fehlen (Akkoladenwechsel)
287	Vl		< Beginn gem. **AM**, **RV**
288, 290	Vl		> Ende gem. **RV**
289	Vl		**SP**, **OP**: < Beginn zw. *a* und Taktstrich

2. Satz

36–37	Vl		**AM**: < fehlt; **SP**, **RV**, **OP**: erst ab Zz. 4
	Pf		**AM**: < fehlt; in **SP**, **OP** unterschiedlich; NA → Vl
70, 72	Pf		**AM**: < fehlt; in **SP**, **OP** unterschiedlich; NA → Pt. 62, 64
77	Vl	2–4	**OP**, **OV**: *stacc.*-Pkte. fehlen
111–112	Vl		< gem. **RV**
125–126	Pf		< Beginn gem. **SP**
133–134	Pf		< in den Quellen uneinheitlich; NA → Pt. 125–126
136	Pfo	1–2	**OP**: Hbg. *fis'–fis'* fehlt, vgl. auch T. 144, 152
141–142	Pf		**AM**: < fehlt; in **SP**, **OP** unterschiedlich; NA → Pt. 149–150
154–155	Pf		**AM**: < fehlt; in **SP**, **OP** bis T. 154 Ende; NA → Vl, vgl. auch T. 155–156
188–189	Pf		< in den Quellen unterschiedlich; NA: → T. 190–191
190–191	Vl		< gem. **AM**, **RV**
	Pf		< in den Quellen unterschiedlich; NA: → Vl

3. Satz

76–78	Pf		< gem. **SP**
85	Vl		**OP**: > bereits ab T. 84 Ende
87–89	Pf		**AM**: < > fehlen; in **SP**, **OP** unterschiedlich; NA → **OP** T. 87
118	Vl		> Ende in allen Quellen unterschiedlich; in NA korr.

4. Satz

2	Pf		**AM**, **OP**: < fehlt; **SP**: T. 1–10 Textverlust; NA → Pt. 6, 107
6	Vl		**AM**, **OP**, **OV**: < erst ab 2; NA → **SP** T. 107
	Pf		**AM**, **OP**: < unterschiedlich; NA → **SP** T. 107
22, 23	Pfo		< > in den Quellen unterschiedlich; NA → **AM** T. 22
26, 27	Pf	Zz. 4	**OP**: > als > zw. den Systemen; NA → **SP** T. 127f.
32, 34	Vl		**OV**: > als > unter der jeweiligen Note
37	Pf	Zz. 3	*dim.* in den Quellen unterschiedlich; NA → Pt. 136, Vl
39–40	Pfo		**SP** p. rev., **OP**: Lbg. fehlt; NA gem. **AMR**
41	Vl		**OP**: > Zz. 1–3
	Pf		> in den Quellen unterschiedlich; NA → Vl
41–42	Pf		**OP**: < Beginn Zz. 4+; NA gem. **AMR**, **SP** p. rev.
43	Pf		**OP**: > nur Zz. 2 – Zz. 3, 2. ♪; NA → Vl
58	Pfo OS	Zz. 2	𝄽 gem. **AM**
60	Vl		**OV**: < Zz. 2–4
68, 70	Vl	Zz. 2, 4	**OP**: < > jeweils zentriert zu 2. ♪
69	Vl		**OP**, **OV**: < erst ab 2. Note; NA → Pstn., **SP**, **RV**
69, 103	Pf		< in den Quellen unterschiedlich; NA → Pt. 2, 6, Vl
71	Pf		**AM**: < fehlt; in **SP**, **OP** unterschiedlich; NA → Pstn.
86, 87	Vl		**OP**: < Ende jeweils zw. 5 und 6; NA gem. **SP**, **OV**
90	Vl		**OP**: < Zz. 3–4; NA gem. **RV**, **OV**
91	Vl		**OV**: < Beginn zw. Zz. 2 und 3; **OP**: Zz. 3–4; NA gem. **RV**
95, 103	Vl		**OV**: < ab Zz.1+
101	Pfu		**SP**, **OP**: Bg. nur zu Zz. 4; NA: Bg. ab Zz. 2, letztes ♪ (analog der ursprünglich beabsichtigten Bogenführung)
107	Vl		**OV**: < erst ab 2. Note
	Pf		**OP**: < erst ab 2. Note; NA gem. **SP**
123	Pfo		**OP**: < erst ab Zz. 2+; NA gem. **AM**, **SP**
	Pfu		**OP**: *nicht gebunden* erst Zz. 2; NA korr. gem. **OP** Pt. 22
124	Pfo		**OP**: < erst ab Zz. 2+; NA → T. 123
125	Pfo		**OP**: *nicht gebunden* erst Zz. 1, 4. ♪; NA → T. 24
128	Pf		*stacc.*-Str. gem. **SP**
132, 139	Pf		< in den Quellen unterschiedlich; NA → T. 31, 40

138–139	Pfo OS		**OP**: Bg.-Anfang fehlt (Seitenwechsel), NA gem. **AMR**, **SP** p. rev.
140	Vl		**OP**: > Zz. 1–3
	Pf		> in den Quellen unterschiedlich; NA → Vl
146	Pf		**OP**, **SP** p. rev.: < fehlt; NA gem. **AMR** Pt. 47
154	Vl	5	**OP**, **OV**: > statt ∧; NA gem. **SP**, **RV** Pt. 156
157	Vl		**OV**: < Zz. 2–4
158	Vl		**AM**, **RV**: < fehlt; sonst unterschiedlich; in NA korr. nach T. 157 / **AM**, **RV**: <;
160	Pfu		< gem. **SP**
164	Pfu		**OP**:  ; NA gem. **SP**
177	Vl		**OV**: < erst ab Zz. 1+
179	Vl		**OV**: < erst ab 2
180	Vl		**OP**: < Beginn zw. Zz. 1 und 2, Ende zw. Zz. 3 und 4
	Pfo		**OP**: Bg. bis l.N.; NA gem. **SP**
180–181	Pf		**AM**: < fehlt; in **RV**, **OP** Zz. 2–3; NA → Vl
181	Vl		**OP**: < erst ab Zz. 2
	Pfo		**OP**: Bg. 1–8; NA gem. **RV**

CRITICAL NOTES

Abbreviations

acc.	according to
a. rev.	before revision
b.	bar(s)
bt.	beat(s)
btw.	between
err.	erroneously
l.n.	last note
l.s.	lower staff
l.v.	lower voice
NA	the present edition
pf	pianoforte (both staves)
pfu	pianoforte (upper staff)
pfl	pianoforte (lower staff)
PN	plate number
p. rev .	after revision
p.p.	parallel passage(s)
p.b.	parallel bar(s)
resp.	respectively
stacc.	*staccato*
vn	violin
u.s.	upper staff
u.v.	upper voice
→	adopted to

1st Violin Sonata, op. 105

Sources

AM Autographical working manuscript (Düsseldorf, 12th–16th September 1851). Complete text of the 3 movements including numerous discarded text fragments, corrections and instructions for Robert Schumann's copyists. Paris, Bibliothèque Nationale, Département de la Musique, Ms. 331.

OP, OV Original edition: piano score (**OP**) and separate violin part (**OV**). Published by Friedrich Hofmeister, Leipzig, January 1852. PN: 4508. *Sonate / (in A moll) / für / Pianoforte und Violine / componirt von / ROBERT SCHUMANN / Op. 105. Pr. 2 Thlr. / Eigenthum der Verleger / Eingetragen ins Vereins Archiv. / LEIPZIG, BEI FRIEDRICH HOFMEISTER. / Paris bei S. Richault. ... London bei Ewer & C°*
Zwickau, Robert-Schumann-Haus; archive no.: 94.41a/b – D1.

PR,VR Piano score and separate solo part of the edition by Simon Richault. Presumably published in Paris, 1853. PN: 12.602. R.
Paris, Bibliothèque Nationale, Département de la Musique, Ms. VM 15 5345.

Evaluation of sources and the edition

The sources provide only an incomplete documentation of the genesis of the work. Only the working manuscript (**AM**), the authorized original edition (**OP, OV**) and the piano score with the solo part published by Simon Richault in Paris (**PR, VR**) have been passed on. There are no copies serving as engraver's copies (cf. Schumann's instructions for the copyists in **AM**) or proofs. Discrepancies between **AM**, **OP** and **OV** show that Schumann made corrections during the printing stage. Corrections must have been made in the lost copies of the separate solo part and in the violin part of the piano score which were not checked against each other. Evidence of this is supplied by discrepancies between **OV** and the solo part in **OP**. It is assumed that **OV** was engraved following the copy of the solo part including the corrections which were not taken over in the copy of the piano score. In contrast, the copy of the score was the basis of the violin part in **OP**.

This means that the original edition, the composer's authorized final version, is the principle source. In this edition, the piano part follows **OP**; where discrepancies exist between **OP** and **OV**, the violin part follows the more differentiated version. **AM** was consulted in the case of variants and contradictory readings in order to determine the correct reading. In places where the edition follows **AM**, the deviations in **OP** and **OV** are mentioned in the Detailed Notes. If it was not possible to clarify the divergences between **OP** and **OV** by consulting **AM**, the more differentiated version was given preference or the most plausible version was selected on comparing the parallel passages. In such cases the source of reference (**OP** or **OV**) is not explicitly mentioned in the Detailed Notes. Divergent readings of parallel phrases that are unmistakably intended by Schumann as reprises, have been usually standardized with preference to the more detailed version. However, in particular cases, where there are valid reasons for doing so, the edition retains the discrepancies in dynamics and articulation. Where there are discrepancies in the use of *staccato* dots and strokes, this edition uses *staccato* strokes when in doubt. Parallel passages in **AM** and the authorized original edition, particularly in the third movement, show that Schumann obviously did not distinguish clearly between dot and stroke; however, in b. 198 of **OV**, he corrected *staccato* dots to *staccato* strokes. With regard to the method of notating consecutive slurs and ties, the present edition – in contrast to the new edition of the complete works of Schumann – follows the notation of the original edition.

Additions by the editor to the musical text are indicated by square brackets. Cautionary accidentals added by the editor are not indicated by brackets.

In the Detailed Notes the format: bar – staff / voice – symbol (note or rest) and beat resp. – comment is used.

Detailed Notes

1st movement

vn: < or > acc. **OV**: b. 4, 15, 84–85, 110–111, 112, 118, 205

2	vn		**OP, OV**: *cresc.* missing; NA → pf, **AM**
10	pf		**OP**: < from bt. 2+
17	pf	bt. 1–6	**OP, AM**: 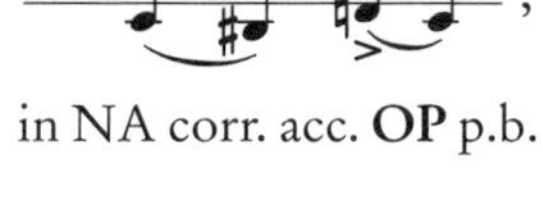 ; in NA corr. acc. **OP** p.b. 131

19–22	vn		**OP**: *cresc.* form b. 19, bt. 1, continuation lines missing
	pf		**AM**: continuation lines for *cresc.* missing; in **OP** to end of b. 21; NA → vn
29	pf		**AM**: < missing; **OP**: < from bt. 5; NA → p.b. 143
36, 150	pfu u.v.	bt. 4	**AM**: ♪ (*b′* and *g′* resp.) and tie missing; **OP**: bt. 3–4 *b′* and *g′* resp. as ♩; NA → vn and b. 40 and 154 resp.
47–49	vn		> varying in the sources; NA: beginning acc. **OP**, end acc. **OV**
	pf		< : **AM, OP**: b. 47, bt. 4 – end of b. 47, >: **AM**: b. 48, bt. 3–6; **OP**: b. 48 bt. 1–5; NA → vn
51–52	pfu u.v.	bt. 4–6	**OP**: slurs missing
55	pf		**OP**: ***f*** not until b. 56, 1
57	vn	bt. 6	**OP**: ♯ on *c″*♯ missing
59–60	pfl		in **AM** not written out; **OP**: slurs b. 59, bt. 4 – b. 60, bt. 3 in 2 parts (change of line); in NA corrected acc. u.s., b. 61–62, 173–174
63–64	vn		**OP**: transposing an octave of **AM** not carried out
66	vn	2	**AM, OP, OV**: ♫; NA → b. 2
		bt. 4–6	**OP, OV**: with slur; NA acc. **AM** b. 2
68	vn		> acc. **AM**; **OP**: > 2–3;
69	pfu u.v.	bt. 3–4	**AM, OP**: *c″* ♯ as ♩; NA → b. 70
75	pfu	bt. 4–6	**OP**: u.v. and l.v. swapped
76	pfu	bt. 5	**OP**: *stacc.* dot missing
78	pfu	bt. 4	**OP**: ♭ before *b′* ♭ err. in the 3rd space
79	pfl	bt. 3	**OP**: ♮ for *f* err. before *g*
80	pfl	bt. 4	**OP**: ♯ for *c*♯ missing, extant not until bt. 6
85	vn		**AM**: > missing; **OP, OV**: diverging; NA → pf
	pfl		**OP**: ***f*** instead of ***sf***; NA → **AM** b. 87
86–87	pf		**OP**: < > under l.s.; NA → b. 84–85
94	vn		**OP, AM**: *cresc.* btw. *e″* and *g′*
105	pfl l.v.	bt. 5	**OP**: 𝄿 instead of 𝄾
106	vn		**OP**: *cresc.* only after bt. 1
108	pfu	1	**OP**: ♩ instead of ♪
110, 114	pf		**OP**: ✻ after bt. 5; NA → b. 111–112
113–115	vn		tie acc. **OV**
124	pf		**OP**: < from bt. 1+; NA → **AM** p.b. 10
133–136	vn		**OP**: *cresc.* from b. 133, bt. 4, continuation lines to end of b. 133; NA → **OV** p.b. 19–22
	pf		**OP**: continuation lines for *cresc.* to end of b. 133; NA → p.b. 19–22
141–142	pfu	bt. 4–3	**OP**: quaver stems for l.v. missing
	pfl		**OP**: slur b. 141, l.v. 2 – b. 142, l.v. 3; NA → p.b. 27–28
145	pfu	bt. 4–6	**OP**: u.v. and l.v. swapped, slur on semiquavers (= u.v.); NA corrected acc. p.b. 31 and **AM**
145–146	pf		**AM, OP**: ***sf*** above u.s.; NA → b. 32–33, 147
158	pfu	bt. 4–6	**OP**: ; NA → **AM**, p.b. 44
161–163	vn		**OP, OV**: < varying; NA acc. source for the repeat passages in **AM**
	vn		> varying in the sources; NA → p.b. 48–49
	pf		**AM**: < > missing in the source for the repeat passages; **OP**: < b. 161, bt. 4–6, > b. 162, bt. 1–6; NA → vn
163	vn		**OP**: ***p*** missing
165–166	pfu u.v.	bt. 4–6	**OP**: slurs missing
168	pf		**AM**: ✻ missing; **OP**: ✻ btw. bt. 4 and 5; NA → p.b. 54
	pfu		**OP**: slur bt. 1–6; NA → p.b. 54
169	pf		**OP**: ***f*** not until b. 170
186, 188	pfu	bt. 1–3	**AM**: slurs missing; **OP**: slur on l.v.; NA → vn
189–190	vn		fingering acc. **OV**
198	pf		**AM**: *cresc.* missing; **OP**: btw. bt. 3 and 4; NA → vn

2nd movement

2	pf		**OP**: *rit.* btw. bt. 1 and 2; NA acc. **AM**, vn
5	pfu	2	**OP**: 𝄾 instead of 𝄿
5–6	pfl		**AM**: slur ends beyond end of bar; **OP**: slur b. 5, 3–5; NA → pfu
8, 33	vn	5	**AM, OP**: with *stacc.* dot; NA → b. 9–10, **OV**
9	vn	10	**OP**: with *stacc.* dot; NA → p.b. 34, **OV**
10, 35	vn	1	**OV**: ***sfp*** instead of >
13–14	vn		**OP, OV**: tie *b–b* missing
14			*rit.* varying in the sources; NA → p.b. 2, 7, 39
27	vn		**AM**: < 2–6; **OP, OV**: < missing; NA → p.b. 2
28	vn		**AM**: > b. 27. l.n. – b. 28, 1; **OP, OV**: > missing; NA → p.b. 3
30–31, 61–62	pfl		**OP**: slur b. 30, 3–5; NA → pfu
35	vn	3–4	**OP**: *stacc.* dots missing
38–39	vn		**OP, OV**: tie *b–b* missing
45	vn	1	**AM, OV**: ***f*** missing
47–48	vn		**AM**: slur missing; **OP**: 2 slurs: 1st slur b. 47, 1–4, 2nd slur b. 48 1–3; NA acc. **OV**
56	vn		**AM**: ***p*** instead of *dim.*; **OP, OV**: *dimin.* btw. bt. 1 and 2; NA → pf
58	pfu	1	**OP**: vs. ♪ instead of ♬
63	vn		< 2–6 acc. **OV**
64	vn	3–4	*stacc.* dots acc. **OV**
65	vn	6–8	slur acc. **OV**

66	pfu	3	**OP**: err. ♯ before e′♭, ♭ vor f′♯
67	pf		**AM**: *dim.* missing; **OP**: *dimin.* btw. bt. 1 and 2; NA → vn
77–78	vn		slur to b. 78, 1 acc. **OV**

3rd movement

vn: < or > acc. **OV**: b. 31–32, 36, 54–55, 87–88, 90–91, 108, 157
vn: *staccati* acc. **OV**: b. 8, 13, 58a/b, 129, 180, 189, 191 u. 201: always on 1st note; b. 204 on l.n.

2	pf		**OP**: < to b. 3, 1; NA acc. p.b. 18, 118, 134, **AM**
13	vn	1, 4	**OP**: *stacc.* dots corr. to *stacc.* strokes (p.b. 129, however, *stacc.* dots); NA acc. **OV**
18	vn		**OP**: < to b. 19, 2; **OV**: < to b. 18, l.n.; NA → p.b. 2
27–28	pf		**AM**: Ped., * missing; **OP**: * after b. 27, l.n.; NA → p.b. 143sq.
29	vn	2	***p*** acc. **OV**
31–32	pfl		**OP**: b. 32: end of slur missing; **AM**: slur in b. 32 only
40	vn	5	**OP**: additional *stacc.* dot; NA acc. **OV**
46	pfu		**OP**: slur missing
55–56	pfu		**AM**, **OP**: slur to b. 54, l.n. only
	pfl		**OP**: slur missing
61	vn		*cresc.* from bt. 1 acc. **OV**
65, 66	vn	1, 4	ʌ acc. **OV**, cf. also b. 69, 71, 73–74
84–86	vn		**OP**: < b. 84, bt. 2 – b. 85, 1 (3rd triplet quaver); **OV**: 1st < b. 84, bt. 2 – b. 85, bt. 1 (2nd triplet quaver), 2nd < b. 86, bt. 1 – b. 87, bt. 1 (change of line); NA: corr. < b. 84, bt. 2 – b. 87, bt. 1
	pf		**OP**: 1st < b. 84, bt. 2 – b. 85, l.n., 2nd < b. 86, bt. 2. – end of bar; NA → vn
107	vn		**OP**: *cresc.* on 2nd instead of 3rd note
109	vn	4	**OP**: *stacc.* stroke and *stacc.* dot engraved over one another without deleting the original version; **OV**: *stacc.* stroke instead of *stacc.* dot; NA acc. p.p. b. 112–114, **AM**
111	vn	4	**OP**: ***p*** instead of ***pp***; NA acc. **OV**
117	vn	4	**OP**: *stacc.* stroke and *stacc.* dot engraved over one another without deleting the original version; NA acc. **OV**
118–119	vn		< varying in the sources; NA: beginning acc. **OV**, end acc. **OP**
121–122	pf		**OP**: < not until b. 122 (= b. 6 of the source for the repeat passages of **AM**: change of line and page turn resp.); NA → p.b. 5–6
124	vn	1	*stacc.* dot acc. **OP** p.b. 8
129	pfl	1	**OP**: ʌ on u.s. 1; NA → p.b. 13, **AM**
137	vn	1	ʌ acc. **AM** p.b. 21
143	pfu	1	**OP**: additional ʌ
	pfl	1	**OP**: *stacc.* dot instead of *stacc.* stroke
144	pf		**AM**: * missing; **OP**: * btw. 3rd and 4th ♪
147	vn	1	***f*** acc. **OV**
150–151	pfu		**OP**: originally *stacc.* dots, *stacc.* strokes engraved over them without deleting the original version
	pfl		**OP**: *stacc.* dots instead of *stacc.* strokes; NA → u.s.
162	vn		**OP**, **OV**: *cresc.* after bt. 1; NA → p.b. 46, **AM**
168	vn		**OV**: *4te Saite* not until b. 169, 1; NA → **OP**, 1st movement, b. 1
172–173	vn		**OP**, **OV**: < > missing
177	vn	5	fingering acc. **OV**
185	pf		**OP**: Ped. already b. 184, bt. 2+
186–187	pf		**OP**: * b. 186–187 bt. 2+; NA: b. 185–187 pedal notation standardized
188	vn	1	**OP**: ʌ; **OV**: *stacc.* stroke; NA → b. 189–192
192	vn	1	***f*** acc. **OV**
202–203	vn		**OP**: *stacc.* dots instead of *stacc.* strokes; NA acc. **OV**
205	pfu	1	**OP**: *stacc.* dot missing
209	pfu	1	**OP**: *a″* missing

2nd Violin Sonata, op. 121

Sources

SK Sketches for the 1st movement of the piano score (Düsseldorf, no later than 26th October 1851).
Zwickau, Robert-Schumann-Haus, archive no.: 10398 – A1.

AM Working manuscript, extant in two separate parts.
Part 1: complete text of movements 1–4 (Düsseldorf, 26th October – 4th November 1851). Bifolio subsequently added with a new version of the piano accompaniment to the 4th movement, b. 35–51 (= **AMR**).
Part 2: discarded version of bars 62–94 of the 4th movement (Düsseldorf, 29th October – 2nd November 1851).
Düsseldorf, Heinrich-Heine-Institut, accession no. 74.118 and 97.5046 G.

SP, RV Engraver's copy of the original edition of the piano score (**SP**) and fair copy of the separate violin part (**RV**), (Düsseldorf, 4th – 15th November 1851). Copyist: Peter Fuchs, source: **AM**.
SP: Copy of 1st – 3rd movement (up to b. 129) and b. 11–185 of the 4th movement. A single sheet with b. 130 – 140 of the 3rd movement and b. 1 – 10 of the 4th movement is lost. Gaps in the musical text because of corresponding instructions by Robert Schumann

and illegibility of passages in **AM** which were repeatedly corrected (e.g. violin part, 1st movement, b. 1 – 6, deleted by R. Schumann in **AM**, later restored by Clara Schumann).
Two revised versions: completion by R. Schumann of the gaps in the copy left by Fuchs, correction of errata, addition of ties and slurs, dynamic and articulation marks, also amendments to draft in the second revised version. Thereafter also repeated corrections by R. and Cl. Schumann (incl. new version of b. 35 – 51 and 134 – 150 in the 4th movement) based on the new version of the piano part in **AM**. Numerous additions by Clara Schumann, particularly at the parallel passages not written out by R. Schumann in **AM**. Entries added by an unknown hand. Final revision by R. Schumann (*Revised / d. 13.10.52*). Numerous entries by the engraver.
RV: Fair copy made from **SP**, but not identical with the violin part in **SP**.
Changes made by R. Schumann during revision. Moreover, additions and corrections by Cl. Schumann, Wilhelm Joseph von Wasielewski (first performer of the solo part) and possibly also by Ferdinand David, who also played from **RV**. Also fingerings, presumably by Wasielewski (particularly in the 4th movement), cautionary accidentals and enharmonic notation (with ♯) of b. 97 of the 4th movement to make reading easier. Changes and additions in **SP** and **RV** during run-through, not compared in both parts.
Carpentras, Bibliothèque Inguimbertine, MS 1071.

OP, OV Original edition: piano score (**OP**) and separate violin part (**OV**). Published in September 1853 by Breitkopf & Härtel in Leipzig. PN: 8761.
2te. / GROSSE SONATE / FÜR / Violine und Pianoforte / FERDINAND DAVID / zugeeignet / VON / Robert Schumann. / Op. 121. / Eigenthum der Verleger. / Leipzig, bei Breitkopf & Härtel. / Pr. 2 Thlr. 15 Ngr. / Eingetragen in das Vereinsarchiv. / 8761. / Entd. Sta. Hall.
Düsseldorf, Robert-Schumann-Forschungsstelle, Sammlung Fink, Inv. no.: 911

Evaluation of sources and the edition

The abundant quantity of sources documents the genesis of the work almost completely. However, the copies **SP** and **RV** contain various revisions which were not compared. Nevertheless, **SP** undoubtedly served as the engraver's copy for the original edition (**OP** and **OV**). **RV** was not the engraver's copy for **OV**, but still had an indirect influence on the presentation of the original edition, as the violin part in **OP** and **OV** includes additions and corrections inserted in **RV**. The comparison of the differences existing between the copies must have been made during the printing phase, which was supervised by Schumann himself. However, the actual process of engraving of the violin part can no longer be reconstructed, as the proofs have been lost. Numerous adjustments were also made in the passages in **OP** and **OV** which were marked by Schumann in **AM** as repeats. However, these amendments are missing in the copies. Thus it appears that Schumann was still changing the notation during the printing phase.

In consequence, the original edition (**OP** and **OV**) is the principle source for the present edition. Although this is the authorized final version by Schumann himself, for the critical revision of the musical text it is necessary to refer to earlier stages in order to transform contradictory readings into the right one. In these cases, the engraver's copy **SP** must be consulted in particular as a reference source for this edition. **AM** is them included when **SP** is also insufficient for determining the correct version. Where this is not possible, parallel passages are compared and the most plausible version is chosen in each case. Numerous variants in parallel passages that are unmistakably intended by Schumann as reprises have been usually standardized with preference to the more detailed version.

With regard to the method of notating consecutive slurs and ties, the present edition – in contrast to the new edition of the complete works of Schumann – follows the notation of the original edition.

Additions to the musical text made by the editor are marked in square brackets. Cautionary accidentals added by the editor are not indicated by brackets.

The following Detailed Notes document the differences between the principle source and the present edition. Inaccuracies in the principle source relating to articulation, dynamics or pedalling, which arose through lack of space, are corrected in this edition without comment. In the 1st movement in **OP**, for example, b. 6, 31, 33, 114, 119–120, 129–130, 139, 145, 149–150, 199 each have *Ped.* before the note to be pedalled, in b. 91 of the 3rd movement after the note; and in b. 17 of the 1st movement, the *dim.* in the violin and pianoforte was engraved after the point at which it was supposed to begin. Wherever the violin parts of **OP** and **OV** do not coincide, the invalid variants are mentioned in the Detailed Notes but the source of reference is not mentioned again. In the Detailed Notes the format: bar – staff / voice – symbol (note or rest) and beat resp. – comment is used.

Detailed Notes

1st movement

7–8	vn		< > varying in all sources; NA acc. **AM**
8	pf		* on bt. 2 acc. **SP**
24	pfl	1	*stacc.* stroke acc. p.b. 192
		bt. 4+	*arpeggio* sign acc. p.b. 192
25	vn		**OP**:  ; OV: < > on *e'*; NA acc. **RV**
27	pf		**AM**: *Ped.* missing
31, 199	pfl u.v.	bt. 1	𝄾 acc. **OP**
45–46	pf		> different in the sources, in p.b. 109–110, 113–114, 119–120, 125–126, 213–214 as well; in NA end of > always regulated acc. b. 45–46
57–58	vn		< > acc. **SP, RV, OV**
60	vn		**OV**: < > centered between bt. 1 and 2
72	vn		< acc. **SP**

128	pf	1	**OP**: ***sf*** missing
169	vn	2	**AM**: *a♭*; **SP, RV**: err. *b♭♭*; error adopted in **OP, OV**
213	pf		**SP, OP**: ***p*** not until bt. 1+; NA → p.b. 45, **AM**
224	vn		**OP**: 1st slur 2–6 instead of 2–7
226	vn		**OV**: > bt. 1–3
229–230	vn		< > acc. **OV** (compared to p.b. 61 notation changed, but possibly no difference in interpretation was intended)
238–239	pf		**AM**: no pedal notation in the source for the repeat passages b. 226–250, which were not written out; **SP, OP**: pedal notation varies; NA: pedal notation acc. **OP** (notation changed compared to p.b. 70–71, but possibly no difference in interpretation was intended)
240	pf		**OP**: < already from bt. 2+; NA acc. p.b. 72, **SP**
247	vn		**OP**: slur 4–8 instead of 3–8
249	vn, pf		**OP**: *cresc.* bt. 1+; NA → p.b. 81, **OV, SP**
285–286	pfl		**OP**: ties missing (change of line)
287	vn		< beginning acc. **AM, RV**
288, 290	vn		> end acc. **RV**
289	vn		**SP, OP**: < beginning btw. note *a* and barline

2nd movement

36–37	vn		**AM**: < missing; **SP, RV, OP**: from bt. 4 only
	pf		**AM**: < missing; in **SP, OP** varying; NA → vn
70, 72	pf		**AM**: < missing; in **SP, OP** varying; NA → p.b. 62, 64
77	vn	2–4	**OP, OV**: *stacc.*-dots missing
111–112	vn		< acc. **RV**
125–126	pf		< beginning acc. **SP**
133–134	pf		< varying in the sources; NA → p.b. 125–126
136	pfu	1–2	**OP**: tie *f'*♯ – *f'*♯ missing, cf. also b. 144, 152
141–142	pf		**AM**: < missing; in **SP, OP** diverging; NA → p.b. 149–150
154–155/	pf		**AM**: < missing; in **SP, OP** to end of b. 154; NA → vn, cf. also b. 155–156
188–189	pf		< varying in the sources; NA: → b. 190–191
190–191	vn		< acc. **AM, RV**
	pf		< varying in the sources; NA: → vn

3rd movement

76–78	pf		< acc. **SP**
85	vn		**OP**: > already from end of b. 84
87–89	pf		**AM**: < > missing; in **SP, OP** varying; NA → **OP** b. 87
118	vn		end of > diverging in all sources; corrected in NA

4th movement

2	pf		**AM, OP**: < missing; **SP**: b. 1–10 text lost; NA → p.b. 6, 107
6	vn		**AM, OP, OV**: < only from 2; NA → **SP** b. 107
	pf		**AM, OP**: < varying; NA → **SP** b. 107
22, 23	pfu		< > varying in the sources; NA → **AM** b. 22
26, 27	pf	bt. 4	**OP**: > as > btw. the staves; NA → **SP** b. 127f.
32, 34	vn		**OV**: > as > under the note in question
37	pf	bt. 3	*dim.* varying in the sources; NA → p.b. 136, vn
39–40	pfu		**SP** p. rev., **OP**: slur missing; NA acc. **AMR**
41	vn		**OP**: > bt. 1–3
	pf		> varying in the sources; NA → vn
41–42	pf		**OP**: < beginning on bt. 4+; NA acc. **AMR, SP** p. rev.
43	pf		**OP**: > only bt. 2 – bt. 3, 2nd 𝅘𝅥𝅯; NA → vn
58	pfu u.v.	bt. 2	𝄽 acc. **AM**
60	vn		**OV**: < bt. 2–4
68, 70	vn	bt. 2, 4	**OP**: < > always centered on the 2nd 𝅘𝅥𝅯
69	vn		**OP, OV**: < only from 2nd note; NA → p.p., **SP, RV**
69, 103	pf		< varying in the sources; NA → p.b. 2, 6, vn
71	pf		**AM**: < missing; different in **SP, OP**; NA → p.p.
86, 87	vn		**OP**: end of < always btw. 5 and 6; NA acc. **SP, OV**
90	vn		**OP**: < bt. 3–4; NA acc. **RV, OV**
91	vn		**OV**: < beginning btw. bt. 2 and 3; **OP**: bt. 3–4; NA acc. **RV**
95, 103	vn		**OV**: < from bt.1+
101	pfl		**SP, OP**: slur only on bt. 4; NA: slur from bt. 2, last 𝅘𝅥𝅯 (analogous to the slurring originally intended)
107	vn		**OV**: < only from 2nd note
	pf		**OP**: < only from 2nd note; NA acc. **SP**
123	pfu		**OP**: < only from bt. 2+; NA acc. **AM, SP**
	pfl		**OP**: *nicht gebunden* not until bt. 2; NA corr. acc. **OP** p.b. 22
124	pfu		**OP**: < only from bt. 2+; NA → b. 123
125	pfu		**OP**: *nicht gebunden* not until bt. 1, 4th 𝅘𝅥𝅯; NA → b. 24
128	pf		*stacc.* stroke acc. **SP**

132, 139	pf		< varying in the sources; NA → b. 31, 40
138–139	pfu u.v.		**OP**: beginning of slur missing (page turn), NA acc. **AMR**, **SP** p. rev.
140	vn		**OP:** > bt. 1–3
	pf		> varying in the sources; NA → vn
146	pf		**OP, SP** p. rev.: < missing; NA acc. **AMR** p.b. 47
154	vn	5	**OP, OV:** > instead of ^; NA acc. **SP, RV** p.b. 156
157	vn		**OV:** < bt. 2–4
158	vn		**AM, RV:** < missing; otherwise diverging; in NA corrected acc. b. 157
160	pfl		< acc. **SP**
164	pfl		**OP**: ; NA acc. **SP**
177	vn		**OV:** < only from bt. 1+
179	vn		**OV:** < only from 2
180	vn		**OP**: beginning of < btw. bt. 1 and 2, end btw. bt. 3 and 4
	pfu		**OP**: Bg. to l.n.; NA acc. **SP**
180–181	pf		**AM:** < missing; in **RV**, **OP** bt. 2–3; NA → vn
181	vn		**OP:** < only from bt. 2
	pfu		**OP**: slur 1–8; NA acc. **RV**

WIENER URTEXT EDITION

Werke für Streicher und Bläser mit und ohne Klavier

J. S. BACH

UT 50002 2 Sonaten für Violine und Basso continuo BWV 1021, 1023
UT 50018/19 6 Sonaten für Violine und Cembalo, 2 Bände BWV 1014–1019
UT 50255 Sonaten und Partiten für Violine solo BWV 1001 – 1006
UT 50133 Suiten für Violoncello solo BWV 1007–1012
UT 50260 Suite I für Violoncello solo G-Dur BWV 1007

BEETHOVEN

UT 50017 Variationen über Volksweisen op. 105 / op. 107 für Klavier (und Flöte ad lib.)
UT 50247 Sonaten für Violoncello und Klavier (mit Violoncello-Fassung der Hornsonate op. 17)

BRAHMS

UT 50015 Sonate für Klavier und Klarinette (oder Bratsche) f-Moll op. 120/1
UT 50016 Sonate für Klavier und Klarinette (oder Bratsche) Es-Dur op. 120/2
UT 50011 Sonate für Klavier und Violine G-Dur op. 78
UT 50012 Sonate für Klavier und Violine A-Dur op. 100
UT 50013 Sonate für Klavier und Violine d-Moll op. 108
UT 50039 Sonate für Klavier und Violoncello e-Moll op. 38
UT 50040 Sonate für Klavier und Violoncello F-Dur op. 99

CORELLI

UT 50235/36 Violinsonaten op. 5, 2 Bände

DEBUSSY

UT 50173 Syrinx „La Flûte de Pan“ für Flöte solo

DVOŘÁK

UT 50162 Sonatine G-Dur op. 100 für Violine und Klavier
UT 50244 Werke für Violoncello und Klavier

FRANCK

UT 50174 Sonate für Violine und Klavier

HÄNDEL

UT 50264 Sonaten für Violine und Basso continuo

MOZART

UT 50032–34 Sonaten für Klavier und Violine, 3 Bände
UT 50069 Variationen für Klavier und Violine

REINECKE

UT 50242 Undine, Sonate für Flöte und Klavier op. 167
UT 50263 Undine, Sonate für Klarinette und Klavier op. 167
UT 50272 Sonaten für Violoncello und Klavier

F. X. RICHTER

UT 50189 Sonaten für Flöte (Violine), Cembalo und Violoncello

SCHUBERT

UT 50089 Sonate für Klavier und Violine D-Dur D 384 (op. 137/1)
UT 50004 Sonaten für Klavier und Violine
UT 50087 „Trockne Blumen“ für Klavier und Flöte D 802 (op. post. 160)

SCHUMANN

UT 50237/38 Sonaten für Violine und Klavier, 2 Bände

TELEMANN

UT 50187 12 Fantasien für Flöte solo

VIVALDI

UT 50175 Sämtliche Sonaten für Violoncello und Basso continuo

Die Reihe wird fortgesetzt / This series will be continued

600S IX/2010

Printed in Germany · WEGA Mainz IX/11